The DesLoges Family

NOW

DELOACH

DELOACHE

DELOATCH

Joseph Earle Steadman

HERITAGE BOOKS
2012

HERITAGE BOOKS

AN IMPRINT OF HERITAGE BOOKS, INC.

Books, CDs, and more—Worldwide

For our listing of thousands of titles see our website
at
www.HeritageBooks.com

A Facsimile Reprint
Published 2012 by
HERITAGE BOOKS, INC.
Publishing Division
100 Railroad Ave. #104
Westminster, Maryland 21157

Originally published 1981

International Standard Book Numbers
Paperbound: 978-0-7884-5445-5
Clothbound: 978-0-7884-9220-4

FOREWORD

The main purpose of this book is to show the origin of the DesLoges-Deloache family and, by a series of sketches, to show the direct line of descent of the Reverend Zebulon DeLoache and his children from the first known ancestor. Data on collateral lines generally has been omitted with the thought that full information can or will be included in family records compiled by descendants in those lines.

This book is dedicated to the memory of my deceased wife, Sarah/Sallie DeLoache Steadman, who was a kind, gentle, patient, and loving person, and a faithful wife and mother.

Gratitude is expressed to my nephew, Paul Matheny DeLoache, for having this book published.

Joseph Earle Steadman
3107 Oakdale Road
West Columbia, S.C. 29169

CONTENTS

COAT OF ARMS

Deslages
(De Loach)

THE DesLOGES FAMILY
(Now DeLoach-DeLoache-DeLoatch)

IN EUROPE

As a foreword, all readers hereof are urged to distinguish between the surnames DeLoche and Desloges. The former is pronounced "Duh Loash", while the latter is pronounced "Duh Lozsh". These surnames represent two separate and distinct families of ancient and modern France, and have different origins and meanings. The following information is given concerning the DeLOCHE family.

DELOCHE

The DeLoche pedigree and arms are illustrated and described in "L'Armorial Et Nobiliarie De L'Ancien, Duché De Savoie", a copy of this reference being contained in the Congressional Library at Washington, D.C. The pedigree chart shows several disconnected branches of this family represented during the period of 1307-1894. One branch, traced from the year 1405 through the year 1852, includes representatives who became members of the nobility with titles such as: — Seigneurs De Servoz, Coseigneurs De Bozei, Barons De St. Martin, Comtes De Vanzy, etc. The pedigree chart further shows that this family was settled in the town (or city) of Maglans, Faucigny District of the Duchy of Savoy, prior to the year 1307 and continuously thereafter for several generations. In view of such early and continuous residence in this locality the national origin of the DeLoche family can be determined by reference to the history of the Duchy of Savoy. That history is briefly set forth in the following paragraph.

In the year 1111 Amadeus II, member of a princely family of Northern Italy, was given the title COUNT OF SAVOY when his dominions were raised to the status of a county and received the name of SAVOY. In 1391 Amadeus VIII, a later member, was given the title DUKE OF SAVOY when the family dominions were raised to the status of a duchy (or dukedom). Except for short periods of time the Duchy of Savoy continued to be a part of the Italian States during the following 469 years. In 1860 it was ceded to France, and is now divided into the present day departments of Savoie and Haute Savoie in Eastern France. The above-mentioned Faucigny District is a territorial division of Haute Savoie.

From the preceding paragraph it will be seen that the DeLoche family of the Duchy of Savoie is of Italian origin rather than French origin. The pedigree chart shows that the family name in Latin was DeOCHIA (or DeHOCHIA). The derivation of this surname and the transition to its present form is explained by A. Dauzat on page 188 of his Etymological Dictionary of Family Names and Christian Names of France — (Dictionnaire Etymologique Des Noms De Famille Et Prénoms De France), as follows:

> Deloche, forme du centre, "de l'oie". Voir Deloye (surnom d'un Marchand d'oies, etc.) — Deloche Centre.

The French word "oie (oies)" in the feminine gender is equivalent to the English word "goose (geese)". Therefore the literal meaning of the above is that the form of spelling the name of the center (market) at which geese were sold was altered from "de l'oie" to "de l'oche", and that the latter form eventually became the surname (DeLoche) of a merchant who engaged in business at a goose market. The surname DeLOYE had a similar origin. — (For example: — The name JEAN de l'oche, the original form for JEAN DeLOCHE, literally meant "Jean of the Goose Market".) — The French language is directly descended from Latin, and has dialect differences in different localities of the country. In the Spanish language (also directly descended from Latin) the word for "goose" in the feminine gender is "oca", this being similar to "Ochia" in the previously mentioned Latin surname DeOCHIA.

DesLOGES

The following references show the derivation of the surname DesLOGES, together with the social status and place of residence of this ancient family in France.

Pages 188 and 197 of A. Dauzat's aforesaid Etymological Dictionary of Family Names and Christian Names of France.

Desloges, nom relatif a' un nom de domaine, Loge (primitivement "berceau de feuillage", allemand Laube); aussi nom de village, surtout de hameau.

DesLoges; "(Maison) des loges" (au sens ancien "abri de feuillage", "cabane"), ou "originaire des Loges", nom de localité (de meme origine), répander surtout dans l'Ouest et le centre.

Pages 192 and 216 of Dionne's Origine Des Familles (Origin of Families).

Desloges - Loges, Seigneuries en Bourgogne, en Normandie, et dans le Poitou. Loge, abri de feuillage, cabane, boutique, tribune.

Desloges - Les Loges, Seigneuries en Normandie et dans le Poitou. Loge, abri de feuillage, cabane, boutique, tribune.

The French word "loge" is equivalent to the German (allemand) word "Laube" and the English word "lodge". The above references show that in primitive and ancient times the loge was a cradle (berceau) or shelter (abri) of foliage (feuillage). In later times this word designated a cabin (cabane), a shop (boutique), or a raised platform (tribune). At some date in early history a collection of loges constructed in a certain locality (localité) was called "Les Loges (The Loges)", that name being given to this hamlet (hameau) and its particular locality. The hamlet eventually grew into a village (village) which, with its surrounding lands, became the domain (domaine) of a member of the nobility. This nobleman lived in a castle erected within his domain, and was known as the Lord of Loges (Seigneur Des Loges). The domain was designated as the Lordship of Loges (Seigneurie Des Loges), and the nobleman's children and their descendants were known as the House of Loges (Maison Des Loges). The said references mention the Lordships of Loges in Burgundy (en Bourgogne), in Normany (en Normandie), and in Poitou (dans le Poitou), these being political divisions of the land area of ancient France. It is stated that the DesLoges family was scattered especially in Western and Central France (répandu surtout dans l'Ouest et le centre).

Though the above references mention three Lordships of Loges it is probable that there was only one, that one having been created as a fief in ancient Burgundy at a time when the northwestern corner of that kingdom (or province) extended into Central France. This fief evidently was situated within a geographical area which later, as the lines of political divisions were altered during the course of years, was incorporated into Normandy, next into Poitou, and finally into Touraine. Burgundy was founded as an independent kingdom by the Burgundians, a German tribe which settled in the southeastern third of the country in the year 413, and continued as such during many years before becoming a part of modern France. As is suggested by one of the above references, the name of the fief might first have been "Laube", a German name which became Gallicized into "Loges" when the area was merged into France. It appears that the particular area was that which lies to the south of the present city of Orleans. Maps which define the political divisions of the territory of ancient France in the year 800 show that parts of Burgundia, Neustria (became Normandy in the year 912), and Aquitania (the northern part became Poitou prior to 1189) border on each other at about twenty-five miles southeast of Orleans. At about the year 1661 the eastern part of Poitou was formed into the Province of Touraine.

The "Old Lordship of Loges in Touraine (Desloges-Tour. Vieux Seigneurie)", together with a description and/or an illustration of the coat armor of the DesLoges family, is mentioned in the following references.

> Page 1233 of Reitstap's Armorial General, Vol. 2 (L-Z), 1887. — (The same description is given in the 1903 and 1904-1914 editions of this reference.)
> Desloges (Tour): D'azur a' une tour d'arg., maconnée de Sa., soutenue d'un Croiss du sec.

Since the Province of Touraine was formed in the year 1661, it is evident that the Lordship of Loges in that province was existent in the said year. It is interesting to note from history that the average Frenchman then represented a nation whose people were the product of the earlier welding together of several tribes into one. The earliest known inhabitants of ancient France were the Celts, who were living there as early as the year 630 B.C. During the centuries from about 630 B.C. to about 912 A.D. the Celts became amalgamated, successively, with invading and conquering tribes of the Cimbrian, Roman, and Teutonic peoples. We are thus informed as to the racial origin of the DesLoges family.

The rise of Protestantism, embracing the doctrines of Martin Luther and John Calvin, began in France in the sixteenth century. Of all the kings who ruled there from 1515 to 1715 only Henry IV (1589-1610) favored the cause of the Protestants. Due to the political and religious character of the opposition launched against them the Protestants became welded together into something like political as well as religious unity, and were termed "Huguenots" by their enemies. The Huguenots were objects of bitter and violent persecution by the Roman Catholic Church and its agents, the disfavoring kings being among those agents. Records of the time show that members of the DesLoges family were actively associated with the Huguenots.

3

Desloges
Tour VS

The above illustration is shown in "Planches Par Roland", Planche CXCIV - Desloges (Tour. Vieux Seigneurie). The following is an illustration of a bookplate from the books or library of Deloges of Burgundy.

DESLOGES. — *Bourgogne.*

EX LIBRIS
DESLOGES

D'azur au lion d'argent.

(Ex-libris).

4

The "Caen Protestant Church Registers", - Volume 1 (1571 and 1572) was the only one available to this writer, - show Estienne Desloges, his wife Marie, and other persons of the same surname as members of that church. Caen (now the capital city of the department of Calvados) then was a city in the old Province of Normandy. It was on 24 August 1572 that the terrible "Massacre of Saint Bartholomew" began in Paris. During the thirty days of slaughter, which spread throughout France, some 70,000 to 100,000 Huguenots lost their lives.

In 1624 the Duke - Cardinal Richelieu became the head of affairs in France and began a crushing warfare against the Huguenots, whose rallying point then was the fortified city of Rochelle (now the capital city of the department of Charente - Inférieure). This city then was yet in the large Province of Poitou. As stated by Goodrich in his "History of All Nations", during the progress of the war "many of the sturdy Protestant families of Poitou took refuge in Rochelle and were cut off in the celebrated siege and sack of that city, - an event which took out of France a large part of its best blood". The siege of Rochelle lasted from about 1 August to 29 October 1628, and more than 22,000 persons died within the city. It was from Rochelle that some members of the DesLoges family fled to England after revocation of the Edict of Nantes.

The Edict of Nantes was revoked by Louis XIV on 18 October 1685. This edict had been issued by Henry IV on 30 April 1598 and, among other things, provided that the Huguenots have free exercise of religion and equal claim with the Roman Catholics to all offices and dignities. Revocation of the edict deprived the Huguenots of their civil rights and inaugurated a period of persecution, torture, and murder designed to compel them to abjure their faith. By this act more than 500,000 Huguenots were driven out of France and went to other countries, leaving practically all of their material wealth behind them. Members of the DesLoges family were among those who went to England; and some of them, who fled from the city of Rochelle as previously mentioned, became affiliated with the French Church on Threadneedle Street in the city of London. Their names are recorded in the registers of that church and some of the entries concerning them, as appear in Publications of the Huguenot Society of London, are shown (in English translation) below for example.

(1) Adrian Lafons, young man, native of Rochelle, son of Raimond Lafons and Elizabeth Tibau, and Marguerite Desloges, native of Rochelle, daughter of Nicholas Desloges and Marie Eviellard, announced their intention of marriage, 11 December 1687.

(2) On 16 February 1688 Adrian Lafons and Marguerite Desloges were married by Mr. Satur, Minister. Announced in the Church of London. Certificate 15 February, signed by Gravisset.

(3) Marie Desloges, young woman, of Rochelle, 23 years of age, recognized as a member, 14 June 1688.

(4) Marie Desloges, born 8 February -----, married 27 February 1725-6.

(5) Isaac Mordant, widower, native of Hautretop in Normandy, married Elizabeth LaFond, native of London,

daughter of the late Adrian LaFond and the late Marguerite Desloge, 18 May 1730.

While the earliest register entry mentioned above was made in the year 1687, Smiles (the author), in his book entitled "The Huguenots", states that the French church which first was on Threadneedle Street and later removed to Founders Hall Chapel was active during the period of 1599-1753. He also states that the records of most of the Huguenot churches were lost, those which were not lost being now preserved at Somerset House. Therefore, it is understood that the Publications of the Huguenot Society of London contain entries only from those registers which were not lost.

From another source it is learned that one Michael DesLoges was in England in the year 1663, this being thirty-five years after the siege and capture of Rochelle in 1628. The said Michael was born about the year 1645. If his birth occurred in France he fled that country and went to England before or during 1663. If his birth occurred in England it is probable that his parents fled from France during the years of persecuting warfare which followed the capture of Rochelle. His name appears on page 13 of a record entitled "Servants To Foreign Plantations, Vol. II, 1663-1679", as published in a book entitled "Bristol and America - A Record Of The First Settlers In The Colonies Of North America, 1654-1685". In 1663 or 1664 he was registered (as Michaell Deloge) for passage in a ship sailing from Bristol, England, to the Virginia Colony in North America. Regular navigation across the Altantic Ocean from England to the North American Colonies was first established, and then was in continuance at Bristol; therefore Michael's presence at that port can thus be accounted for. He probably went there from London. The author of "Bristol And America" states that though these "Servants of the Plantations" were officially known as such, this name was a misnomer in the majority of cases. The vast majority went out as free emigrants paying the cost of their own transportation and the cost of transportation for others who went with them as their "headrights". It is assumed that Michael paid the cost of his own transportation, since no subsequent mention of him as a "headright" in Virginia has been found. In Virginia his surname became Anglicized as Deloach/DeLoach, which form of spelling some of his descendants changed to DeLoache or DeLoatch.

SKETCH NO. 1
MICHAEL DesLOGES
the
IMMIGRANT TO VIRGINIA

Michael DesLoges (ca. 1645 - lvg. 1709), founder of the DeLoach - DeLoache - DeLoatch family in America, arrived in Virginia from Bristol, England, during the year 1663 or 1664. He then was an unmarried man of about nineteen years of age. He settled in Isle of Wight County, where he became engaged in the business of tailoring. It is conjectured that his parents and/or grandparents owned and operated a tailoring establishment in France or England, and that Michael served an apprenticeship in that establishment before coming to Virginia for the purpose of bettering his lot among the people of that then flourishing colony. As a newcomer to the colony he received a grant of fifty acres of land, but its location has not been determined by this writer.

At about 1668 Michael married Jane Griffith (b. ca. 1650), the only child of Rowland Griffith who — if not a native of Wales — was of Welsh descent. On 9 April 1663 Governor Francis Morrison of Virginia granted to Rowland Griffith 765 acres of land situated on Blackwater River in Isle of Wight County. By his will (9 August 1671) Rowland Griffith of Isle of Wight County gave "all of my estate to Jane Desloges my only daughter now wife unto Michaell Desloges, taylor"; but they were not to sell it. Robert Kae and Charles Williams were appointed as trustees. — (Isle of Wight County, Va., Wills, etc., Book 1, page 238.) The estate included the said 765 acres of land, which doubtless descended to one or more children of Michael and Jane.

It appears that Michael and Jane settled in that part of Isle of Wight County which then was called Newport (or the Upper) Parish, and that he was living there as late as 1709. On 20 June 1709 Thomas Cook of the Upper Parish conveyed to Michael DeLoach of the same parish, for the sum of 2500 pounds of tobacco, 100 acres of land lying in the Upper Parish on the Second Swamp. — (Deed Book 2, page 110). Two days later, on 22 June 1709, his son Michael DeLoach and wife Mary of Warwicksqueake (or the Lower) Parish sold to Jacob Harvey land lying in the Lower Parish. — (Deed Book 2, page 109.)

Michael and/or Jane might have died shortly before or during 1719. The number of children born to them is not known. There probably were one or more daughters who married but, due to the loss of records, now cannot be identified as members of the family. Also, there probably were one or more children who died before reaching the age of maturity. However, records of the time which escaped loss or destruction furnish circumstantial evidence (which has been accepted as proof) that they were the parents of three sons who grew to maturity, married, and left surviving children. These sons were the following named persons.

1. Michael DeLoach, Jr. (ca. 1671 - 1727). — He married Mary _____, and they were the parents of Michael III and Thomas, as named in their father's will. — (Isle of Wight County, Va., Will Book 3, page 38.)

7

2. William DeLoach (ca. 1678 - 1747). — See SKETCH NO. 2.)

3. Thomas DeLoach (ca. 1680 - 1748). — He married _____, and they were the parents of Samuel, Thomas, William, Solomon, and a son (Richard?) who died before the making of his father's will. — (Isle of Wight County, Va., Will Book 5, page 117.) In 1980 Mrs. Ernest Rae Wiese (nee O'Levia Neal Wilson) of Waco, Texas, was gathering data for a record to be published concerning him and his descendants.

SKETCH NO. 2
WILLIAM DeLOACH

William DeLoach (c. 1678 - 1747). — On 9 November 1698, being then a resident of Isle of Wight County, Va., he deposed as to the oral will spoken by his landlady, Margaret Wilson, who died interstate on 16 February 1698. At the time of the deposition it was stated that he was about 20 years of age; therefore, it is evident that he was born about 1678. — (Isle of Wight Will Book 2, pages 386-7.)

At about 1701 William married Eleanor Collins (c. 1683 - 1750), daughter of John and Eleanor (Oliver) Collins of Isle of Wight County. By his will of record in that county John Collins devised to his daughter Eleanor 1,750 acres of land which had been granted to him in Southwark Parish of Surry County, Va., — 800 acres prior to 20 April 1684 and 950 acres on that date. In early 1705 William and Eleanor DeLoach were living on the said land, parts of which they sold at various times, as follows:

(a) 800 acres sold to William Rowland on 5 March 1705. — (Surry County Deed Book 4, page 346.)

(b) 350 acres sold to Thomas King on 14 February 1720. — (Surry County Will and Deed Book, 1715-1730, Part 1, page 317.)

(c) 100 acres sold to Zachariah Madera on 15 April 1723. — (Idem, page 630.)

(d) 500 acres sold to Peter Fiveash on 18 April 1727. — (Idem, page 694.) It was on this tract of land that William and Eleanor lived during their residence in Surry County.

On 21 November 1704 William bought from Debora Portis (widow of John Portis) 100 acres of land lying on Freshpond Branch in the Lower (Warwicksqueake) Parish of Isle of Wight County. — (Isle of Wight Deed Book 2, page 17.) On 5 January 1708 he sold this land to his brother Michael DeLoach, Jr., and Eleanor his wife released her dower rights. - (Idem, Book 2, page 99.) It is probable that William and Eleanor had decided to settle on this land, but soon after its purchase they reversed their decision and moved to the forementioned land in Surry County.

In the year 1719 William and Eleanor sold land to Thomas Day. — (Virginia Historical Genealogies, page 2.) This land doubtless was situated in Isle of Wight County. It might have been a proportionate part (255 acres) of the 765 acres granted to Rowland Griffin/Griffith on 9 April 1663 and devised by him to his daughter Jane Desloges (wife of Michael 1st), which land they were not to sell. — (Other sons, Michael and Thomas, also would have received 255 acres each. It appears that Jane might have died at about 1719; having survived her husband.)

When the last portion of land in Southwark Parish of Surry County was sold (on 18 April 1727) William and Eleanor were living in Isle of Wight County. The deed for the sale states that they "lately lived" on that land. The removal to Isle of Wight County probably occurred in 1723, for in that year he was granted 350 acres of land on the south side of Meherrin River in Isle of Wight County. — (Grant Book 10, page 261; Virginia County Records, Vol. 7, page 8.) In 1732 he was granted an additional 50 acres of land, thought to have been adjoining the said 350 acres. — (Grant Book 14, page 165.) These 400 acres were situated in that part of Isle of Wight County which in 1720 was incorporated into the newly formed Brunswick County and which in 1781 became a part of the present Greensville County. Though Brunswick County was formed in 1720, because of its sparse population the political affairs and public records of the county were administered in Isle of Wight County during the period of 1720-1732. — (Executive Journals of the Council of Coonial Virginia, Vol. IV, page 266.) The said 400-acre tract also bordered on the Virginia-North Carolina boundary line. In connection with the survey of that line it was mentioned on 20 September 1728 as William DeLoach's plantation. — (North Carolina Colonial - State Records, Vol.   , page   .)

North Carolina land grants show that William DeLoache patented lands in that province as follows: — 200 acres in Edgecombe County on 30 June 1738, 400 acres in Bertie (later Northampton) County on 7 May 1742, 600 acres (in two tracts of 300 acres each) in Edgecombe County on 11 November 1743. — (North Carolina Records, Vol. 4, pages 332, 619, and 641; Grant Book 5, page 230; Grant Book 10, page 73.) At some time before his death he gave the 800 acres of land in Edgecombe County to his son William, Jr. By his will he gave the 400-acre tract in Bertie (later Northampton) County to his son Francis. Edgecombe County was formed from the original Bertie County and then included several of the modern counties of North Carolina. — (Corbitt - Formation of North Carolina Counties, 1663-1943.) The exact location (as to modern county) of the land given to William, Jr., has not been determined. However, it is thought that the land was situated either in the present day Warren or Halifax County.

The will of William DeLoach of Brunswick County, Va., dated 25 March 1745 and proved on 3 March 1747, is recorded in Brunswick County Will Book 2, page 140. By this will he disposed of his estate in the following manner.

To his wife Eleanor he gave 500 acres of land (the plantation whereon I now live together with the lands thereunto belonging) for the term of her natural life, two female negroes to be at her own disposing, and a negro boy during the term of her natural life.

To his son Francis he gave the 500 acres of land and the negro boy which were given first to Eleanor during the term of her natural life, 400 acres of land on the south side of Wild Catt Swamp in Northampton (formerly Bertie) County, N.C., and four negroes.

To his daughter Martha (wife of Harmon Hill) two negroes and a chest with key thereto.

To his daughter Anne (wife of William Hill) three negroes, two cows, and two calves.

To his granddaughter Cela Hill (daughter of William and Anne Hill) one cow and calf.

To his son William two negroes. — In times past he had "already given William lands and negroes equal in value or surmounting the value of" what in his will was bequeathed to any one of his other children.

The 500 acres given to Eleanor doubtless included the heretofore mentioned 400 acres in Isle of Wight/Brunswick County and an additonal 100 acres joined thereto at a date not known to this writer. The lands given to William, Jr., prior to the making of his father's will, doubtless were the forementioned 200 acres and 600 acres (total of 800 acres) in Edgecombe County, N.C., and a 100-acre tract in the then Brunswick County, Va., which on 22 February 1727 William, Jr., sold to Benjamin Boykin. — (See SKETCH NO. 3.) In addition to the land (a total of 900 acres) given to William, Jr., he also had received a number of slaves previous to the time when his father made his will. Thus his portion of the estate was "equal in value or surmounting the value" of what was given to any other one of his father's children.

The will of Eleanor DeLoach, widow, of Brunswick County, Va., dated 30 September 1748 and proved on 26 September 1750, is recorded in Brunswick County Will Book 2 (1739-1785), pages 185 and 186. By this will she disposed of her personal property in the following manner.

To her son Francis a negro wench, and all other part of the estate not otherwise mentioned.

To her grandson Thomas DeLoach (son of Francis) a negro girl child.

To her granddaughter Eleanor Hill (daughter of Harmon Hill) fifteen shillings current money to buy her a ring.

To her daughter Anne Hill (wife of William Hill) a riding horse and side saddle, a trunk with lock and key and a large bottle in the trunk, and all wearing apparel.

To her granddaughters Celia Philips and Anne Hill (daughters of William and Anne Hill) a negro girl child, but to Anne only if Celia should die without an heir.

To her son William, Jr., twenty shillings current money.

To her granddaughter Eleanor DeLoach (daughter of William, Jr.) fifteen shillings current money to buy her a ring.

The above-mentioned children are not listed in the order of birth. There probably were others who died before their father's will was made. The order of birth apparently was as follows:

1. William, Jr. (ca. 1702; lvg. 1765) — See SKETCH NO. 3.

2. Martha (ca. 1704; bef. 30 September 1748). — She married Harmon Hill and had issue.

3. Anne (ca. 1707; lvg. 1748). — She married William Hill and had issue.

4. Francis (ca. 1710; 1770). — He married **Charlotte** (?) Hart, and settled in Northampton County, N.C. They were the parents of William, Thomas, Michael, Solomon, and Charlotte DeLoach.

OLIVER

John Oliver (died 1655?), maternal grandfather of Eleanor Collins who married William DeLoach, apparently was an immigrant who came to Virginia from England during the middle 1600s. On 2 July 1650 Governor Berkeley granted to him 300 acres of land on Blackwater River in Isle of Wight County. He died while on a trip to England; but before leaving Virginia, on 19 April 1652 he made a will (recorded on 16 June 1655) in which he mentioned his wife Ellen and gave to his son John and two daughters the land on Blackwater River. — (Deed Book 2, p. 79; Will Book 1, p. 93.)

John Collins (see below) who married Eleanor Oliver (older daughter of John) and John Wakefield who married Mary Oliver (younger daughter of John), with the consent of their wives, on 5 January 1666/7 deeded the 300 acres of land on Blackwater River to John Branch. — (John B. Bodie — Historical Southern Families, Vol. II, p. 98.) It appears that John Oliver the brother of these sisters died, unmarried, prior to the date of the said deed.

COLLINS

John Collins (died 1692), father of Eleanor Collins who married William DeLoach, apparently was either an immigrant who came to Virginia from England during the middle 1600s or the son of an immigrant who came at an earlier date. He settled in Surry County, Va., where before or after and during 1684 he acquired a total of 1,750 acres of land. His first wife was Eleanor Oliver (died before 1682), daughter of John Oliver of Isle of Wight County, Va. — (Will and Deed Book 1, p. 93.) She was the mother of Eleanor Collins who married William DeLoach, and probably was the mother of John Collins, Jr., who died prior to 1692 leaving his sister Eleanor as her father's heir at law.

He evidently was a member of the Friends Society (Quakers). On 4 November 1682, at a meeting of men and women Friends in the house of William Bressies in Isle of Wight County, Va., John Collins and Mary Tooke (perhaps a widow) of Surry County propounded their marriage. At a meeting on 8 December 1682, in the house of Thomas Jordan at Chuckatuck in Nansemond County, Va., they again published their marriage. They were married on 14 December 1682 in the house of John Barnes his father-in-law (the father of Mary) in Isle of Wight County. She evidently died prior to 1692, leaving no Collins children. — (Early Quaker Records in Virginia, p. 222, Chapman — Isle of Wight County, Va., Marriages, p. 103.)

An inventory of the estate of John Collins, deceased, was taken at his house in Surry County, and was signed by J. Tooke and other persons on 8 January 1693. The inventory and record of sale were returned to a Surry County Court held on 3 July 1694. — (Surry County Deed Book, 1694-1709, Part 1, pp. 12 and 13.)

SKETCH NO. 3
WILLIAM DeLOACH, JR.

William DeLoach, Jr. (ca. 1702 - lvg. 1765). — He probably was born in that part of old Surry County, Va., which in 1720 became a part of Brunswick County and in 1781 became a part of the present Greensville County, Va. At about 1725 he married Judith Wall (ca. 1707 - lvg. 1755), daughter of Richard and Lucy Wall. Richard's will (dated 29 February 1752 and proved in August 1755) of record in Northampton County, N.C., names his daughter Judith DeLoach. — (Grimes - North Carolina Wills, 1690-1760, page 390; North Carolina Historical and Genealogical Register, Vol. 1, page 516.) William and Judith first settled on a 100-acre tract of land — (lying on Fountains Creek and Meherrin River in the then Brunswick County and immediately above the Virginia-North Carolina boundary line) — which evidently was given to him by his father. On 22 February 1727, after moving down into North Carolina, he sold this land to Benjamin Boykin, and Judith the wife of William DeLoach, Jr., renounced her dower rights. — (Brunswick County, Va., Deed Book 1, page 406.)

On 6 June 1731 William DeLoach, Jr., was granted 350 acres of land situated on the south side of Meherrin River, in that part of old Bertie County, N.C., which in 1741 was formed into Northampton County. — (North Carolina State/Colonial Records, Vol. 4, page 624.) — Hereafter mentioned as William DeLoach.

In 1739 William DeLoach and Richard Wall (William's father-in-law or brother-in-law) were appointed jurors for Bertie-Edgecombe Counties. On 5 February 1740 William DeLoach appeared on the list of jurors for those counties. — (North Carolina State/Colonial Records, Vol. 4, page 524.)

By his father's will he was given two negroes, with the statement: — "I have already given my foresaid son William DeLoach lands and negroes in times past equal in value or surmounting the value of which I have herein bequeathed to any one of my other children and in fore time delivered to him". The lands given to him were the forementioned 100 acres in Brunswick County, Va., and the 800 acres of land in Edgecombe County, N.C. No record of the disposition of the said 800 acres has been found by this writer.

In 1744-5 William moved to the Welsh Tract on the Pee Dee River in South Carolina. In a petition (read and approved on 8 February 1745) presented to the Council of Colonial South Carolina he prayed for a grant of 350 acres of land in right of seven persons (evidently himself, his wife, and five slaves, — 50 acres of land being allowed for each person) included in his family. For the 350 acres he had previously paid to the possessor £100 currency for his good will, although the possessor then had neither a warrant nor a grant for the land. The petitioner also stated his desire to erect a grist mill for serving the people of the Welsh Tract. The following described actions resulted from this petition.

    (a) On 22 January 1747 William received a grant for 200 acres on the Pee Dee River and situated in the present Chesterfield County, S.C., at a point between the towns of Society Hill and Cheraw. This was his home plantation until

13

20 March 1754, when he sold it and moved to land on the "South Prong" of Lynches Creek in the present Kershaw County, S.C. — (Plat Books, Vol. 4, page 338, Grant Books, Vol. 4, 1752-1774, Class 1, page 116; Council Journals of Colonial South Carolina; H.T. Cook - Rambles In The Pee Dee Basin of South Carolina, page 64; Deed Book PP, pages 269-271, at Charleston, S.C., and microfilm of same in the State Archives at Columbia, S.C.)

(b) On 13 September 1746 a plat for 150 acres on the Pee Dee River and situated in the present Marlboro County, S.C., was certified for William. He either allowed his warrant for the land to lapse or sold it to another person and no grant was given to him. — (Plat Books, Vol. 4, page 339; Council Journals of Colonial South Carolina.)

On 23 March 1748 a survey of 50 acres of land in the present Chesterfield County, S.C., was certified for William, which land apparently was due him in right of a child who came with him to South Carolina and died there during 1745 or early 1746. Since no grant was given to William, he probably sold his warrant for the land to Robert Williams for whom the plat was certified on 5 May 1752. — (Plat Books, Vol. 5, page 169; Council Journals of Colonial South Carolina.)

After coming to South Carolina William and Judith DeLoach became members of the Welsh Neck Baptist Church located at James' Neck, on the Pee Dee River, in the present Marlboro County. At about 1754 a group of members moved westward from this church towards Lynches Creek, where on 1 September 1755 they organized the first Baptist church on that creek. William and Judith went with that group and were constituent members of the said church, which was located on the east side of the main stream of the creek in the present Chesterfield County. — (Leah Townsend — South Carolina Baptists, 1670-1805, pages 95 and 96n.)

On 22 January 1756 and on 9 September 1756 separate plats, — each for 150 acres of land due him in right of three children who came with him to South Carolina, — were certified for William. The said land — (a total of 300 acres for six children) — was situated on the "South Prong" of Lynches Creek in the present Kershaw County, S.C. Since no grants were given to William, he probably sold his warrants for the separate tracts of land, respectively, to William Welsh for whom the first plat was certified on 2 February 1762 and to Andrew Baskin for whom the second plat was certified on 1 December 1761. — (Plat Books, Vol. 7, pages 162 and 188; Council Journals of Colonial South Carolina.)

Early in 1759 many members of the Baptist Church on Lynches Creek removed to Coosawhatchie, where on 12 September 1759 a Baptist church was constituted. This church (now Beach/Beech Branch Baptist Church) was located at the head of the Coosawhatchie River in the present day Hampton County, S.C. It is thought that William and Judith became members of this church. (Leah Townsend — South Carolina Baptists, 1670-1805, pages 47, 48, 95 and 96; Two Centuries of Lawtonville Baptists, 1775-1975, pages XX and 15.) Hampton County then was part of old Granville County, S.C.

On 2 October 1759 William petitioned the Council of Colonial South

Carolina for a grant of 100 acres of land in Granville County. At that time, — because of disturbed conditions attending the Cherokee Indian War of 1759-1760, — no land was surveyed for him. On 6 August 1765 he petitioned that a warrant to him for the land be prolonged. The petition was read and approved, but no record of further action on the matter has been found by this writer. It is believed that William died during or soon after 1765. The requested land apparently was situated in that part of old Granville County which now is Allendale County, S.C. — (Council Journals of Colonial South Carolina.)

On 21 October 1754, prior to his removal to Lynches Creek, William DeLoatch of Pee Dee, Craven County, S.C., gave power of attorney to Arthur Bryan of the same place to receive, recover, — all moneys, — due him in the government of Virginia. — (Records at Charleston, S.C., Courthouse: — Miscellaneous Records, 1754-1758, page 106.) This writer has not determined what moneys were due to William in the government of Virginia, unless the moneys were owing to him by persons who were living in Virginia and had bought William's North Carolina lands.

In addition to the seven children who came to South Carolina with William and Judith there were four others who were born after their parents' arrival in the province. The total number of children included the following listed persons.

1. Thomas (ca. 1726 - ca. 1805). — See SKETCH No. 4.

2. William (ca. 1728 - lvg. 1786). — Born in old Edgecombe County, N.C.; apparently never married; settled in old Beaufort District, S.C.; served with the Americans during the Revolutionary War.

3. A child (ca. 1730 - ca. 1746). — Born in old Edgecombe County, N.C.; died in old Craven County, S.C.

4. Hardy (ca. 1735 - c. 1820). — Born in old Edgecombe County, N.C.; married Elizabeth Hart; settled in old Beaufort District, S.C.; served with the Americans during the Revolutionary War; removed to Georgia after 1790. A record of him and his descendants will be published by His Honor, Judge Harry R. DeLoach of Claxton, Ga.

5. Michael (ca. 1740 - ca. 1815). — Born in old Edgecombe County, N.C.; married Elizabeth Rochell?; settled in old Beaufort District, S.C.; served with the Americans during the Revolutionary War.

6. Jesse (1742 - 1817). — Born in old Edgecombe County, N.C.; married Ann _____; settled in old Beaufort District, S.C.; served with the Americans during the Revolutionary War.

7. Eleanor (ca. 1744 - ca. 1780). — Born in old Edgecombe County, N.C.; believed to have been the first wife of Henry King, Sr., and the mother of the Reverend Henry King, Jr. (Baptist Minister), of old Craven County and old Edgefield County, S.C.

8. Averilla (ca. 1746 - lvg. 1783). — Born in old Craven County, S.C.; married (1) Giles Burdett of old Edgefield County, S.C.; married (2) Henry King, Sr., as his second wife. — (See 7 above.)

9. Frances? (ca. 1748 - lvg. 1774). — Born in old Craven County, S.C.; believed to have been the first wife of Wright Nicholson of old Edgefield County, S.C.

10. Elizabeth (ca. 1750 - 1843). — Born in old Craven County, S.C.; married (1) Josiah Allen; married (2) Aaron Etheridge; married (3)

_____ Edwards — (all of old Edgefield County, S.C.). She was about 93 years old when she died.

11. David (1752 - 1815). — Born in old Craven County, S.C.; married Rebecca _____; settled in old Beaufort District, S.C.; served with the Americans during the Revolutionary War.

William and Judith probably had three or four other children who were born and died in North Carolina before their parents removed to South Carolina.

WALL

Joseph Wall (died 1727), grandfather of Judith Wall who married William DeLoach, Jr., apparently was an immigrant or the son of an immigrant who came to Virginia from England during the middle or late 1600s. He settled in Surry County, Va., where in 1704 he was the owner of 150 acres of land. His will (probated on 13 April 1727 and recorded in Surry County) names his children: — James, Joseph, John, Richard (see below), Robert, and Elizabeth. His wife evidently died prior to the making of his will. — (John B. Boddie — Historical Southern Families, Vol. II., p. 99.)

Richard Wall (died 1755) moved to Northampton County, N.C., where he was living at the time of his death. His will (dated 29 February 1752 and probated in August Court 1755), of record in that county, names his wife Lucy and children: — Sampson, Richard, Arthur, Samuel, Judith **Deloatch** (married William DeLoach Jr.), Sarah Boykin (2nd wife of Francis Boykin), Precila Benson, and Jane Lewis. — (North Carolina Historical and Genealogical Register, Vol. 1, p. 511.)

SKETCH No. 4
THOMAS DELOACH

(In this and the following sketches "Saluda County" is used interchangeably with "Edgefield County" to more specifically designate the location of lands, churches, and places of residence.)

Thomas DeLoach (ca. 1726 - ca. 1805). — He was born in that part of old Brunswick County, Va., which in 1781 became a part of the present Greensville County, Va. Soon thereafter he was taken by his parents to old Edgecombe County, N.C., and in 1744-5 he went with them to the present Chesterfield County, S.C. At about 1749 he married Patience Allison (ca. 1732 - ca. 1805), a supposed relative of Andrew Allison who was a justice of the peace for old Craven County, S.C. — (Andrew Allison, a long-time landowner, lived and died in that part of Craven County which now is Richland County, S.C.) — In 1763 Thomas DeLoach, then living in the present Richland County, "made affidavit before Andrew Allison as a witness to the execution of a paper by Abraham Odam and Cibbie his wife", who also were residents of that county. — (Kirkland and Kennedy — Historic Camden, Part One, page 87n; Green — History of Richland County, S.C., pages 30, 64, 92, and 221.) During the period of 1756-1765 the name of Thomas DeLoache (also Delotch) appears as an adjacent landowner on certified plats for other persons. (Plat Books in the State Archives at Columbia, S.C.)

It is noted from the above cited references that the surname of Thomas is spelled DeLoach or DeLoache, which forms are in current use by his descendants who bear that surname. In the remainder of this sketch, and in the remaining sketches contained in this book, the writer will show the surname mostly as DeLoache, though it might be shown differently in records of the time.

At about 1772-3 Thomas moved from the present Richland County to that part of old Colleton County, S.C., which in 1765 became a part of old Ninety Six District, in 1785 became a part of old Edgefield District/-County, and in 1895 became Saluda County. In response to his petition to the Council of Colonial South Carolina for a grant of land in his new location, on 6 April 1773 a precept (writ, or judicial command in writing) was issued for the survey of 400 acres of land for him. The survey was certified for him on 4 May 1773 and the grant to him was signed on 31 August 1774. The grant, given to Thomas DeLoache by George the Third (King of Great Britain), was signed by William Bull the Lieutenant Governor of the Province of South Carolina. The 400 acres were described as follows:

On Red Bank Creek and on Penn Creek, a branch of Little Saludy River in Ninety Six District, bounding north and northeastward on Samuel Everidge's/Etheridge's, Jacob Smith's, and Joseph Hogan's land; south and westward on Mr. Russell's land and land the owner's name not known and part vacant land; and partly encloses a tract of Sanders Walker and a tract of James Davis (Disones).

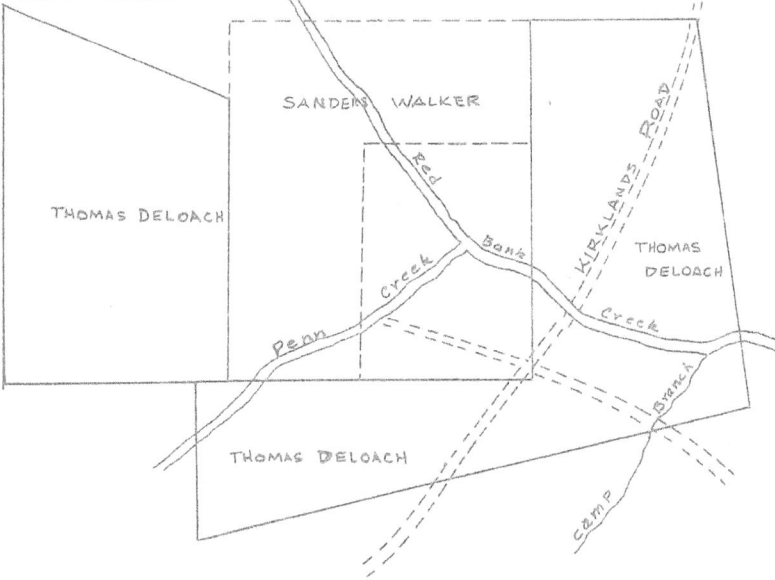

JOSEPH HOGAN

SANDERS WALKER

THOMAS DELOACH

Red Bank Creek

Penn Creek

KIRKLANDS ROAD

THOMAS DELOACH

Creek

Branch

THOMAS DELOACH

Camp

400 ACRES GRANTED TO THOMAS DELOACH 31 AUGUST 1774
RECORDS IN STATE ARCHIVES, COLUMBIA, S.C.
PLAT BOOKS VOL 14 PAGE 366

A record of the above-mentioned grant is contained in the Council Journals of Colonial South Carolina, in a book of Royal Grants (Vol. 32, 1774, Class 1, page 558), and in a book of Memorials (Vol. 13, page 323) in the State Archives at Columbia, S.C. It also is mentioned on page 171 of Leah Townsend's "South Carolina Baptists, 1670-1805"

Records in the courthouse at Edgefield, S.C., show that Thomas DeLoache, Sr., disposed of the foresaid 400 acres of land as follows:

(a) On 7 March 1777 he sold 200 acres to Jesse Jernigan. The witnesses to the deed were Thomas DeLoache, Jr., John Cotton, and Charity Cotton. On 2 September 1785 the deed was proved by Thomas DeLoache, Jr., and recorded on 10 October 1796. — (Deed Book 0/13, 1796-1797, pages 253-257.) On 8 April 1795 the heirs of Jesse Jernigan sold 75 acres of this land to William Burdett. The witnesses to the deed were Henry King, Averilla King, and Joel Brown. — (Deed Book 13, page 247.) On 4 September 1807 William Burdett sold the 75 acres to William H. Lewis, who on 29 December 1813 sold the tract (with other lands) to James Bonham. — (Deed Book JJ/32, page 479.)

(b) On 31 January 1789 Thomas DeLoache, Sr., and his son Michael DeLoache together signed a deed whereby they sold 50 acres to Moses Brown. The witnesses to the deed were Jacob Brown, James Allen, and Christopher Brooks. — (Deed Book 12, 1795-1796, page 23.) It appears that Thomas had previously given the land to Michael, but had not yet given him a covering deed; therefore the son was not free to dispose of the land in his own right. The 50 acres were separated, by a branch, from a tract owned by Michael's brother Samuel DeLoache.

(c) On 12 May 1789 he sold 65 acres to Josiah Thomas. The witnesses to the deed were Henry King, William Burdett, and Samuel DeLoache. The deed was signed by him and his wife Patience DeLoache. — (Deed Book 10, _____-1794, pages 95-97.) This land apparently was a part of the 200 acres which were sold to Jesse Jernigan, but had been recovered by Thomas DeLoache prior to its sale to Josiah Thomas.

(d) The 150 acres remaining after the sales to Jesse Jernigan and Moses Brown apparently were situated a short distance above the junction of Red Bank Creek and Penn Creek. This evidently was the home place on which Thomas and Patience were living at the time of the 1790 and 1800 censuses for Edgefield County, S.C. It is assumed that they died there and were buried in a graveyard on an adjoining plantation belonging to their son Samuel DeLoache. The disposition of the 150 acres has not been learned by this writer.

Thomas and Patience were living alone, and near to their sons Michael and Samuel DeLoache, at the time of the 1790 census for Edgefield County, S.C. At the time of the 1800 census three sons of Michael were living with them. The known children of Thomas and Patience were the following named persons.

1. Michael Allison (ca. 1750; ca. 1800). — See SKETCH No. 4a.

2. Elizabeth (ca. 1752;   ). — At about 1769 she married Barrett Travis as his first wife, and they settled on lands near to her brother Samuel DeLoache in the present Saluda County, S.C. Among their children were the following named persons. — (1790 census for Edgefield County, S.C. — Barret Travis.)

2a. Elizabeth (ca. 1770; lvg. 1830). — She married Mumford Perryman (died 1820). Her uncle Samuel DeLoache was on her bond, as administratrix of her husband's estate, for $30,000.00. After her husband's death she moved to Conecuh County, Ala., where she was reported in the 1830 census for that county. — (Family Records of John B. Boddie, Jr., of Chicago, Ill.; 1790-1820 censuses for Edgefield County, S.C.; Probate Records at Edgefield, S.C.; 1830 census for Conecuh County, Ala.)

2b. Mark (1783-1836). — In 1808 he married Jemimah Stallworth. Their firstborn child was William Barrett Travis (1809; 1836), who was born within four miles of Red Bank Baptist Church in the present Saluda County, S.C., and was killed in the massacre at the "Alamo" in Texas. — (Sarah Sullivan Ervin - South Carolinians In The Revolution, page 135; John A. Chapman - History of Edgefield County, S.C, page 165; Family Records.)

3. Thomas, Jr. (20 October 1759; 29 July 1819). — See SKETCH No. 5.

4. Samuel (ca. 1762; ca. 1845). — See SKETCH No. 4b.

5. Patience (ca. 1765;   ). — In view of her given name and her husband's association with members of the DeLoache family, it is believed that she was a daughter of Thomas and Patience (Allison) DeLoache. At about 1784 she married William Burdett (ca. 1760;   ) who at the time of the 1790 census for Edgefield County, S.C., was living near to Tom (Thomas, Jr.) DeLoache. He doubtless was related to the heretofore mentioned Giles Burdett whose wife was Averilla DeLoache, daughter of William DeLoache, Jr. — (See SKETCH No. 3.) William Burdett and his wife Patience are mentioned in a deed relating to a tract of land which was granted in 1787. — (Edgefield County, S.C., Deed Book 12, 1795-1796, page   .) In 1789 Henry King, William Burdett, and Samuel DeLoache witnessed a deed given by Thomas DeLoache, Sr., to Josiah Thomas. — (Ibid. Deed Book 10, pages 95-97.) In 1795 William Burdett was deeded 75 acres of land (part of 200 acres sold by Thomas DeLoache, Sr., in 1777) by Angelica Jernigan (widow of Jesse Jernigan to whom the land had been sold), James Hart and Elizabeth his wife, Esau Parnell and Angelica his wife, and Kezia Jernigan, heirs and heirs at law of Jesse Jernigan. In 1807 William Burdett deeded the 75 acres of land to William H. Lewis who in 1813 deeded it to James Bonham. — (Ibid. Deed Book 13, page 247; Ibid. Deed Book 32, page 479.)

SKETCH No. 4a
MICHAEL ALLISON DELOACHE

Michael Allison DeLoache (ca. 1750; ca. 1800). — He came to Edgefield (now Saluda) County, S.C., in 1771-2. During the period of 1772-1774 he acquired 550 acres of land situated on Penn Creek, south of Red Bank Creek, and near to his father and brother Samuel. The precept/writ for survey of the first 200 acres for him, dated 5 February 1772, shows his name as Michael or Alas DeLoach, which evidently indicates that his full name was Michael Allison DeLoach. When he sold this land his wife Dorcas DeLoache signed the deed with him. As mentioned in SKETCH No. 4, at a later date he acquired 50 acres of land which were part of the 400-acre tract granted to his father on 31 August 1774. Of the total of 600 acres which he acquired 400 acres were sold to other persons prior to the year 1800. The remaining 200 acres were sold at some time prior to 26 March 1806, probably in settlement of his estate. — (Council Journals of Colonial South Carolina, Plat Books, Land Grant Books, and Memorial Books, in the State Archives at Columbia, S.C.; Edgefield County, S.C., Deed Books 1, 12, 17, and 27 for the period prior to 1807.)

No record of Revolutionary War service has been found for him, since many of the muster rolls and payrolls were lost or destroyed during and after the war.

In 1783 he was one of the bondsmen for the administration of the estate of Giles Burdette, and in 1794 he was one of the witnesses to the deed given by his brother Thomas DeLoache for the sale of land. — (Willie Pauline Young - Abstracts of Old 96 and Abbeville District S.C., Wills and Bonds, page 31; Edgefield County, S.C., Deed Book 29, 1808-1809, page 277.)

It is said that Michael moved from Edgefield County to old Beaufort District, S.C., where he lived for a period of time before and after 1790. He was not listed in the 1790 census for Edgefield County, but two persons of the name Michael DeLoach are listed in the 1790 census for Beaufort District. It is believed that he was one of these persons and the other one was his uncle of the same name. The number of children that he then had (four males and four females), except for a daughter who later married, agrees with the total number of children (four males and three females) included in his family at the time of the 1800 census for Edgefield County.

Michael was twice married, the first wife being the mother of all his children. At about 1777 he married Dorcas Still (ca. 1760; ca. 1795), daughter of John and Jean Still. John's will, dated 26 September 1797, mentions his deceased daughter "Dorkes DeLoche". After Dorcas' death, and before 1800, he married a woman (name not known to this writer) who then was forty-five or more years of age. She was included in the 1800 census for Edgefield County as a member of his household. — The will of John Still is recorded in Edgefield County Will Book A, page 131.

Michael apparently died within one or two days after having been recorded in the 1800 census for Edgefield County and prior to completion of the said census. His two younger sons, in addition to a male in-

21

fant who already was there, were taken into the home of his parents (Thomas and Patience DeLoache) and his other children went elsewhere to live. Of his eight children, apparently born in the following order, the names of only four are known to this writer.

1. Son (ca. 1778; lvg. 1800)

2. Dorcas (ca. 1780; lvg. 1815). — It is believed that she was the person of that name who married Jordan Smith prior to 1800. On 2 January 1815 Dorcas and Jordan Smith deeded to William DeLoache (son of the Reverend Thomas DeLoache) 74 acres of land situated on Clouds Creek of Saluda River. — (Edgefield County Deed Book 34, page 119.)

3. Son (ca. 1782; lvg. 1800).

4. Michael, Jr. (ca. 1784; lvg. 1812). — He was recorded twice in the 1800 census: — first as a member of his father's family, and again as a member of the family of his grandparents (Thomas and Patience DeLoache). He was listed in the 1810 census for Edgefield County, being then married and without children. During the War of 1812 he was a corporal in Juhan's Battalion of South Carolina Militia. — (Records of War of 1812 in the National Archives at Washington, D.C.)

5. Daughter (ca. 1786; lvg. 1800).

6. Daughter (ca. 1788; lvg. 1800).

7. Thomas (ca. 1791; lvg. 1830). — He was recorded twice in the 1800 census: — first as a member of his father's family, and again as a member of the family of his grandparents (Thomas and Patience DeLoache). This writer has not identified him in the 1810 and 1820 censuses. He was listed in the 1830 census for Edgefield County, being then married and the father of seven young children (three sons and four daughters). He and his wife apparently died before 1840, and the census for that year apparently shows his sons living with their DeLoache cousins: — two with F.W. (Floyd?) DeLoache and one with Luellen/Llewelyn DeLoache. These sons either died or moved from South Carolina prior to 1850.

8. Samuel (ca. 1794; lvg. 1870). — He was living with his grandparents (Thomas and Patience DeLoache) at the time of the 1800 census for Edgefield County. His whereabouts at the time of the 1810 and 1820 censuses has not been determined. At about 1824 he married Mary Morse (ca. 1804; lvg. 1870).

On 25 October 1829 Samuel was a purchaser at the sale of the estate of Jonathan DeLoache,· son of Solomon DeLoache who came from Virginia to Edgefield County shortly before 1800. — (Edgefield County Office of Probate Judge, File 8, Pack 288.)

Samuel was recorded in the 1830 through 1870 censuses as the head of a family in Edgefield County. In 1850 he was an overseer for Reuben Bouknight, and in 1860 he was an overseer for W. Bouknight. His children, as shown in census and family records, were the following named persons.

1. Willis (ca. 1825; lvg. 1880). — At about 1849 he married Elizabeth _____ (ca. 1820; lvg. 1880), and they became the parents of the following named children who were born in Edgefield County. — Myra (b. 1850), Catherine (b. 1852), Mary (b. 1853), Martha (b. 1854), Allen (b. 1855), James (b. 1857), Matilda (b. 1858). These children are named in the 1850 - 1880 census records. Nothing further is

known concerning them.

2. Sallie (ca. 1826; lvg. 1840). — No further information.

3. Allen (ca. 1829; lvg. 1880). — At about 1864 he married Matilda Smith (1840; 1896), and they became parents of the following named children who were born in Edgefield County. — Isabelle/Ella (b. 1865), John (b. 1869), Ida (b. 1873), Michael (b. 1876). These children were named in the 1870 and 1880 census records. Nothing further is known concerning them.

4. Martha (ca. 1830; lvg. 1850). — No further information.

5. Samuel, Jr. (ca. 1833; ca. 1869). — He served as a private with South Carolina troops during the War Between the States. — (John A. Chapman — History of Edgefield County, S.C., pages 423 and 435.) At about 1864 he married Mary Ivans (ca. 1844; lvg. 1880), and they became the parents of two children whose names are recorded in the 1880 census for Edgefield County, — Lula (b. 1867) and William/Willie (b. 1868). Nothing further is known concerning them.

6. John (ca. 1836; 1869). — At about 1866 he married Mrs. Mary (Abney) Walton (ca. 1834; lvg. 1880) and they became the parents of two children whose names are recorded in the 1880 census for Edgefield County, — Pope (b. 1867; a daughter, who married Will Clary) and Carrie (b. 1868; married Will Crawford).

7. George (1839-1897). — He served as a private with South Carolina troops during the War Between the States. — (John A. Chapman - History of Edgefield County, S.C., page 498.) At about 1870 he married Lavinia Attaway (1852; 1926), and they became the parents of the following named children who were born in Edgefield County.

7a. Mattie (b. 1871). — She married Oliver Butler and had issue.

7b. James (b. 1873). — In 1896 he married Lola Haltiwanger (1873; 1958), and had issue: — Helen (1897; 1939), married Sumpter Gillian; — Judson, married Ruth Attaway and had issue.

7c. Walter D. (1874; 1946). — At about 1899 he married Susan Turner (1881; 1950), and had issue: — Mattie Lou (b. 1900), married Walter J. Horne; — Emmie (b. 1902), married Olin Bryan; — Elmer Walker (1904; 1974), married Emma Martin and had issue; — Ina (b. 1906), married Steve Gallimore; — Ruby (b. 1908), married 1st Herman Scurry, divorced, and 2nd Marion Lagrone; — Lois (b. 1911), married Victor Shidle; — Heber (b. 1913), married Myrtis Lybrand and had issue; — Sue May (b. 1915), married 1st Lyman Frady and 2nd William Fordson; — Maberline (b. 1916), married Edward Fortner; — Floyd (b. 1919), married Mrs. Lillian (Banks) Burnett and had an adopted son; — Reginald (b. 1921), married Mary Pool and had issue.

7d. Lula (b.   ). — Married William P. Stroud.

7e. Lod D. (1882; 1959). — Married 1926, Mrs. Alma (Walton) Morse - DeLoache (1877; 1968). He had no issue.

7f. George, Jr. (1885; 1927). — Married, 1911, Nancy Bledsoe (1894; 1928), and had issue: — Margaret (b.   ), married Joe Ben Attaway; — Lloyd (1914; 1933), unmarried; — Herman (b.   ); — George (b.   ).

7g. Effie (1887; 1944). — Married Wilber Calloway.

8. William (1840; 1864). — He served as a private with the South Carolina troops during the War Between the States and was killed in bat-

tle on 21 August 1864. In 1861 he married Elizabeth Reames (1848; lvg. 1880) and had issue whose names are recorded in the 1870 and 1880 censuses for Edgefield County, as follows:

8a. Luther (b. 1862). — Married, 1894, Mary Cordelia Rushton, and had issue: — Caleb (b. 1895), married 1st Maggie Goldman and 2nd Ardelia Love; — Annie (b. 1897), married Fred Bridges; — Bertha (b. 1900), married 1st Henry Blue, 2nd a Mr. Miller, and 3rd Asbury Weston; — Floride (b. 1901), married Dillard Compton; — Manuel (b. 1905), married Iline Watts; — W.D. (b. 1908), married Ione Wright.

8b. Webster D./Jeff (1864; 1946). — Married, 1896/7, Virginia Susan Dunn, and had issue: — Arthur William (1897; 1964), married Sarah _____, and they had no issue; — Alvin Bernard (1899; 1951), married Louise _____, and had a daughter; — Bertha Mae (b.   ), married Maynard C. Grayson and had two children (Athlene and Webster D. Grayson).

9. Caleb (1841; 1897). — He served as a private with the South Carolina troops during the War Between the States. — (John A. Chapman - History of Edgefield County, S.C., page 494.) In 1867 he married Nancy C. Attaway (1844; 1897), and they became the parents of the following named children who were born in Edgefield County.

9a. Sophia E. (1868; 1882). — Unmarried.

9b. Fannie Lee (1869; 1917). — Unmarried.

9c. Thomas Avery (1871; 1964). — Married, 1895, Belle Berry (1877; 1970), and had issue — Eloise (died in infancy); — Eunice (b. 1897), married, 1917, W. Rufus Wactor, and had issue; — George Avery (b. 1902), married, 1934, Thelma Louise Minick (b. 1909), and had no issue; — Steven Arno (b. 1904), married, 1928, Mary Elizabeth/Lizzie Minick (1902; 1962), and had an adopted daughter (Patricia) and a son who died at birth.

9d. Elizabeth/Lizzie (b. 1872). — Married James/Jim Salters and had issue.

9e. Joseph Samuel (b. 1874). — Married Annie C. Spivey, and had issue: — Harold, married Sallie Bryant and had issue; — Herman, married _____; — Victor (1909; 1930), married

9f. Hillary D. (1876; 1905). — Married 1st Sallie Chapman (;) and 2nd Mary Williams (1895; 1969) and had issue (six by 1st wife and one by 2nd wife): — A child who died in infancy; — John Lee; — Ira (1910; 1921); — Caleb Eugene (1913; 1970), married Ella Louise Chapman and had issue; — Hillary D., Jr.; — Harvey (1921; 1973), married Rita Black and had issue; — Thomas/Tommy.

9g. James Chesley (1876; 1945). — Married Sophia Cockrell (1880; 1939), and had issue: — Mamie, married R. Lee Rushton; — Annie Bell, married _____ Powell and had issue; — Olla Mae, married Horace Boland and had issue; — Joseph Evans (1909; 1960), married Ollie Morgan and had issue; — Idessa, married _____ Mitchell; — Maude, married Evan Osborn; — Sophia, married Carlton Smith; — Caleb; — Fannie Lee; — James Chesley.

9h. Ola Eustachia (b. 1879). — married 1st Jeff Gilliam and 2nd James/Jim _____ and had issue.

9i. John Pierce (1881; 1884).

9j. Lillian P. (1883; 1884).

9k. Sudie (1886; 1918). — Married James C. Stidham and had issue.

10. Matilda/Tilda (1842;   ).

11. Milledge (1845; 1921). — He served as a private with South Carolina troops during the War Between the States. — (John A. Chapman - History of Edgefield County, S.C., page 494.) He married Sallie Cunningham (1850; 1891), and they became the parents of children (order of birth not shown): — Madge (married George Bladon); — Leila (married Peter Bridget); — Sallie (married Jim Briscoe); — Mollie (married _____ Lewis); — Mattie (married Tilman Rushton); — Marion (married Julia Grayson); — John Pierce (married Bertha Padget); — William D. (married Sallie Christie); — Milledge, Jr. (married Eva Clark); — Melvin/Melve (married _____ McKenny); — Pick (d. 1940; unmarried); — Pope (d. 1880, aged 6 months).

12. Malachi D. (1847; 1921). — He was twice married, his first wife being Rebecca _____ (1850; 1870) who left no issue. His second wife was Susan Bethania/Betty Dodgen (b. 1851), who was the mother of the following named children: — Frances (b. 1871); — James William (1872; 1929), married Lovely Turner and had issue; — John Oliver/Oll (1874;   ), married Ann Palm Leopard (1877; 1942) and had issue; — Barbara (b. 1875), married _____ Wicks; — Alice (b. 1877), married _____ Eidson; — Emma (b. 1879), married _____ Moody; — Ella, married _____ Anderson; — Sophia (d. 1927), unmarried; — Alma (1882; 1917), unmarried; — Eva; — Samuel/Mance, married _____ Young.

SKETCH NO. 4b
SAMUEL DELOACHE

Samuel DeLoache (ca. 1762; ca. 1845). — At about 1772-3 he came with his parents from the present Richland County, S.C., to that part of old Edgefield District which in 1895 became Saluda County, S.C. During the Revolutionary War he served as a private in Captain William Butler's Company of Volunteer State Militia. A payroll of Captain Butler's company shows that during the period of 1 September 1781 - 1 March 1782 Samuel DeLoach (No. 8) served 182 days for which he was entitled to pay. His claim for payment was processed on Return No. 50, and Warrant No. 286 in the amount of 26 £ 1s. 5d. sterling was issued to him on 12 August 1785. — (Revolutionary War Records in the National Archives at Washington, D.C. — Miscellaneous South Carolina Records, Folder No. 9; Janie Revill - Copy of Original Index Book of Revolutionary Claims in South Carolina, page 85; Revolutionary War Records in the State Archives at Columbia, S.C. — File No 1851; Alexander S. Salley - Stub Indents to Revolutionary Claims in South Carolina, Lib. U.) In 1782 a band of Tories under "Bloody Bill" Cunningham, being encamped near Bouknight's Ferry on the Newberry side of Saluda River, was surprised by Captain William Butler's Company of South Carolina Rangers (Volunteer State Militia). As the panic-stricken Tories fled, some of them attempting to cross the river to the Edgefield side, (Samuel) DeLoache raised his gun to shoot, but Captain Butler ordered him to desist, as it was desired only to capture or disperse the Tories. — (John A. Chapman — History of Edgefield County, S.C., page 41.)

In 1788 Samuel witnessed a deed given by his brother Michael and wife Dorcas DeLoache to Thomas Williams. In 1789 he was mentioned as a brother of Michael, in a deed given by the latter to Moses Brown, and he witnessed a deed given by his parents (Thomas and Patience DeLoache) to Josiah Thomas. In 1802 Samuel was a purchaser at the sale of the estate of William Simpkins who died in that year. In 1817 he witnessed a deed given by John Feaster to William DeLoache (son of Thomas DeLoache, Jr.). In 1819 and in 1820 he received payment (authorized by the State Legislature) for service as constable of Edgefield County. In 1820 he proved the will of Mumford Perryman, and was a bondsman for the widow Elizabeth (Travis) Perryman as administratrix of her husband's estate. In 1825 he was an appraiser of the estate of Eliza Burton, who perhaps was his mother-in-law. (Courthouse Records at Edgefield, S.C. — Deeds, Wills, and Administrations; Laws of South Carolina — Acts of the Legislature, 1819 - item 19 and 1820 - item 206.)

Other than in one instance, this writer has found no record of land owned by Samuel DeLoache in Edgefield County. On 19 February 1819 he and his wife Ferriby sold to Sophia Bonham 200 acres of land (excluding ¼ of an acre "where the graveyard is near the creek") on the south side of Red Bank Creek, bounded by Red Bank Creek, Penn Creek, Hardy's Branch, lands of James Hart, Sophia Bonham, Mrs. Mobley, and said DeLoache. Witnesses: - Mumford Perryman and William Foy. — (Deed Book 42, 1826-1827, page 307.) The adjoining lands of Samuel DeLoache have not been identified by this writer, but he probably lived there until about 1826 when he moved to Pickens County,

Ala. He was listed in the 1830 and 1840 censuses for that county.

At about 1787 Samuel married Ferriby **Burton?** (ca. 1765; lvg. 1840) and they became the parents of children, all of whom were born in Edgefield County. Census records for the said county show that during the period of 1790-1820 a total of eleven children were living in his household, though all of them were not there at the same time. It appears that at least eight of these persons were his children, while the other three probably were sojourners. Three of the eight children died in infancy or childhood, leaving two daughters (names unknown to this writer) who probably married young and the following named sons.

1. Samuel, Jr. (ca. 1788; 1827). — At about 1814 he married Mrs. Tirza Crawford (ca. 1790;   ), daughter of William and Sarah (Johnson) Hagood of Edgefield County. — (William and Mary College Quarterly; Margaret Watson - Greenwood County Sketches, page 369.) She was the widow of James Crawford who died leaving daughters Mary (married Thomas DeLoache, a brother of Samuel, Jr.) and Eliza (married William Baldwin). After the death of Samuel, Jr., Tirza married James Chiles and bore two children. — (Letter of Miss Eva Hagood of Greenwood, S.C., dated 3 February 1932.)

On 18 February 1819 Samuel DeLoache, Jr., and his wife Tirza sold to Joseph Stalworth 38½ acres of land lying on "waters of 96 Creek, adjoining Richardson Hagood and being the tract of land that was deeded to James Crawford by William Hagood." Witnesses were: — Mumford Perryman and William Foy. — (Edgefield County, S.C., Deed Book 36, . . . — 1819, page 101.) Tirza probably was a sister of the said Richardson Hagood, and she evidently was a close relative of Governor-General Johnson Hagood who later owned lands near Saluda Old Town, the site of a conference between Indians and South Carolina officials in 1755. — (John A. Chapman - History of Edgefield County, S.C., page 12; Saluda County In Scene and Story, page 6.)

Samuel, Jr., was listed in the 1820 census for Edgefield County as head of a household consisting of himself, 3 males under 10 years of age, 2 females (stepdaughters) 10 to 16 years of age, 1 female (wife) 26 to 45 years of age, and 1 female (mother-in-law) over 45 years of age, and 75 slaves. In 1826 he applied for letters of administration on the estate of Sarah Hagood, his mother-in-law, and for an order to sell her personal property. — (Edgefield County, S.C., Probate Records, Box 13, Pack 371.) In 1827 he, together with one of his sons, died by drowning while swimming in a river and soon thereafter his widow moved to Tuscaloosa County, Ala., where in 1828 she bought land from and sold land to Charles S. Patterson. — (Tuscaloosa County, Ala., Deed Book F, pages 373 and 432; Alabama Records, Vol. 7, pages 15 and 34.)

Samuel Jr., and Tirza were parents of the following named children, all of whom were born in Edgefield County, S.C., — William Wiles (ca. 1815; lvg. 1850. — Moved to Alabama with his mother; married, about 1847, M. Louiza McPhail and in 1850 they were living in DeSoto Parish, La., where he, his wife, and son William E. were included in the census for that year.); — Alfred **Burton?** (ca. 1817; 1827. — In 1827 he, together with his father, died by drowning while swimming in a river.); — James Madison (1820; 1858. — Moved to Alabama with his mother. At about 1841 he married his first wife by whom he had a daughter

Lavenia. In 1844 he married Cornelia Elizabeth Christopher by whom he had children: — James Christopher, 1845; 1904, married Susan Madison Larkins and had issue; — Ann Tillman, 1847; died in infancy; — Mary Elizabeth, 1849; 1925, married the Reverend Samuel Monroe Thames and had issue; — Thomas Henry, born 1850, married Lucy Baltzell and had issue; — John Edwin, born 1852, married Julia Smith and had issue.) — The family of James Madison DeLoache is included in the 1850-1870 censuses for Choctaw County, Ala.

2. Thomas (ca. 1799; 1861). — At about 1820 he married Mary Crawford (ca. 1805; ca. 1826) and settled in Edgefield County, S.C., where he was included in the 1820 census as head of a household consisting of himself, his wife, and (as is believed) two orphaned children of his deceased uncle Thomas DeLoach (Baptist preacher). Mary, who bore him two children, was the daughter of James and Tirza (Hagood) Crawford. At about 1826 he moved to Pickens County, Ala., where in 1829 he married Sarah E. Price (1812; 1894), his second wife, and they were living there at the time of the 1830-1850 censuses. At the time of the 1860 census Thomas and Sarah were living in Choctaw County, Miss., where his son Samuel also then was living.

The children of Thomas and Mary (Crawford) DeLoache were: — Edwin A. (1820; 1864. — At about 1839 he married Mary A. _____ by whom he had children: — William, born 1840; — John E., born 1841; — Sarah E., born 1844; — Nancy C.J., born 1849.) — Thomas G. (1825; lvg. 1896. — At about 1845 he married Louise Manerva _____ by whom he had children: — James, born 1846; — Thomas, born 1848; — John; — William; — Walter; — Edwin.).

The children of Thomas and Sarah E. (Price) DeLoache were: — Samuel (1830; 1909. — In 1858 he married Mary Jane Holland by whom he had children: — Henri Ella, 1860; 1950, married George William Yeates and had issue; — Charles Thomas, born 1862; — William Samuel, born 1865, married Zillah Johnson; — Ada Belle, born 1867; James Edwin, born 1870, married Sue Gains and had issue; — Javis Miller, 1873; 1902, unmarried; — George, 1876; 1876; — Wyatt Findlay, born 1880, married Mary Leech and had issue); — James Madison (1832; 1842); — Martha Jane (born 1835, married Frank Driver and had issue.).

3. James William (1804; 1875). — At about 1826 he moved with his parents to Pickens County, Ala., where he became a Missionary Baptist preacher. At about 1830 he married Mary _____ (ca. 1799; ca. 1847), born in Kentucky, who apparently was a widow with three teen-age children. He settled in Pickens County, where he and his family are included in the 1840-1860 censuses for that county. His death was reported in the February 12, 1875, issue of the Livingston (Alabama) Journal. His known children, as shown by census records and a letter (dated 12 March 1932) from Mrs. Connie Thames Lloyd of Jackson, Miss., were the following named persons. — Frank (ca. 1831; ca. 1849. — He was killed in the gold rush to California.); — Alfred (ca. 1834; ca. 1865. — He was killed in a difficulty with Federal soldiers shortly after the War Between the States.); — Milburn (ca. 1836;   ); — Daughter (ca. 1837;   ); — Daughter (ca. 1842;   ); — William L. (ca. 1844;   ); — James M. (ca. 1846;   ).

4. Mary (ca. 1806;   ).

28

SKETCH No. 5
THOMAS DeLOACHE, Jr.

Thomas DeLoache, Jr. (20 October 1759; 29 July 1819). — At about 1772-3 he came with his parents from the present Richland County, S.C., to the present Saluda (then Edgefield) County, S.C., and lived with them in their home which apparently was situated a short distance above the junction of Red Bank Creek and Penn Creek.

On 7 March 1777 Thomas DeLoache, Jr., John Cotton, and Charity Cotton witnessed a deed given by Thomas DeLoache, Sr., to Jesse Jernigan. This deed was proved by Thomas DeLoache, Jr., on 2 September 1785. — (Edgefield County, S.C., Deed Book O, page 257; Ibid, Deed Book 13, 1796-1797, page 253.)

Thomas, Jr., was thrice married, all of his wives being residents of the Ridge Section of the present Saluda County. At about 1779 he married Mary _____ (ca. 1760, ca. 1801), who is said to have been a Miss Asbill or a Miss Crawford; however, this writer believes that neither of these surnames is correct. Thomas' son Allison DeLoache married a granddaughter of Aaron Asbill and his nephew Thomas DeLoache married Miss Mary Crawford. Census records of 1790 and 1800 for Edgefield County, S.C., indicate that the first wife was the mother of twelve children, four of whom died in infancy or childhood. Eight of these children are named in their father's will. At about 1803 he married Sarah Watkins (_____ August 1780; 9 June 1818), probably a daughter of John Watkins, who bore him nine children whose names are recorded in their parents' family Bible. At about 1805 he moved to Lexington County, S.C., where he acquired land and was listed in the 1810 census for that county as the owner of one slave. Prior to or during 1814 he returned to Edgefield County. Shortly before his death in 1819 he married Mrs. Charity Cotton (widow of the Reverend John Cotton) who bore him no children and who was the administratrix of his estate. The 1820 census for Edgefield County shows her as head of a household including herself and two males (18 to 26 years of age) who are believed to have been the two oldest sons of Thomas' son William DeLoache. She then was the owner of five slaves. In 1823 she was living in Butler County, Ala.

After their arrival in the present Saluda County it is probable that Thomas DeLoache, Jr., his parents, brothers, and sisters became members of the Mine Creek Baptist Church on Mine Creek of Little Saluda River, which was situated a few miles distant from their new home. This church was organized in September 1770 and held its meetings in the home of Benjamin Bell until it was continued or replaced to some extent by Red Bank Baptist Church in 1784. — (Leah Townsend - South Carolina Baptists, 1670 - 1805, page 148.) This DeLoache family evidently moved their membership to the Red Bank Baptist Church, which was located nearer to their homes and with which many of their descendants were affiliated during subsequent years.

Soon after its establishment in the spring of 1790 Thomas, Jr., became a member of Clouds Creek Baptist Church (now West Creek Baptist Church) in the present Saluda County. In 1793 he, as a lay member of that church, was sent as a messenger to the meeting of the Bethel Baptist Association with which the said church was affiliated. In 1793/4 he was licensed as a local preacher, and after the departure of the pastor (Patrick Quartermus) in 1794 he worked among the congregation until June 1800. As a licentiate he represented the church at six association meetings during the period of 1794 - 1800. On 4 June 1800 he was ordained by the Reverends Charles Bussey and Henry King as a full minister of the gospel, and soon thereafter assumed the pastorate of the church. He served the church as pastor continuously during the period of 1800 - 1818, and as a minister or messenger was present at meetings of the Bethel Baptist Association, Edgefield Baptist Association, Savannah River Baptist Association, Charleston Baptist Association, and Sarepta Baptist Association (in Georgia). In 1802 he presented a petition to the South Carolina State Legislature praying for incorporation of the church as a society under the name "The Baptist Church of Christ on Clouds Creek". The petition was granted by Act of 8 December 1802. — (Leah Townsend - South Carolina Baptists, 1670-1805, pages 169-171, 269; Hortense Woodson—History of Edgefield Baptist Association, 1807-1957, pages 21, 22, 78, 81; Laws of South Carolina — Acts of Legislature, 1802, page 70.)

On 5 March 1804, according to call of Clouds Creek Baptist Church, the Reverends John Landrum, Samuel Marsh, Henry King, and Thomas DeLoache met at Dry Creek and established the Dry Creek Baptist Church, situated near the town of Ward in Saluda County. Thomas DeLoache did most of the preaching there until his death in 1819. When he died he was buried in the cemetery at this church, and in 1958-9 his grave was permanently marked by a monument erected by some of his descendants. — (John A. Chapman — History of Edgefield County, S.C., pages 307-308.)

In 1814 the Reverends Thomas DeLoache, Francis Walker, and John Landrum established the Philippi Baptist Church, situated about five miles southeast of the present town of Johnston, S.C., and Thomas DeLoache preached there during the period of 1814-1819. — (John A. Chapman — History of Edgefield County, S.C., page 310.)

The late Mr. Lanis Hite of Johnston, S.C., and New York City found records showing that, up until the time of his death, the Reverend Thomas DeLoache preached at the Flat Rock Baptist Church (founded about 1803 and formerly called Walker's Meeting House), situated two or three miles east of Mount Calvary Lutheran Church, in the extreme eastern section of the present Edgefield County. He also found records of legal citations published by Mr. DeLoache at the churches which he served.

The following is an incomplete record of the real estate transactions of Thomas DeLoache, Jr.

In Edgefield County, S.C.

On 21 October 1794 Thomas DeLoache sold to James Whittle 50 acres of land (part of a tract granted to William Holstein, James Warren, and Hendley Webb on 8 July 1774) bounding north on James Whittle and east on Hendley Webb. The deed was signed by Thomas DeLoache and Mary his wife, and witnessed by Samuel Deen and Michael DeLoache. —

(Deed Book 29, 1808-1809, page 277.) It has not been determined when, how, or from whom this land was acquired by Thomas DeLoache.

On 25 February 1803 Thomas DeLoache bought from Arthur Watson 320 acres of land (part of 420 acres originally granted to Arthur Watson) situated on the road from Augusta to the Ridge, on waters of Beach Creek and on Dry Creek waters of Mine Creek, bounding on Willis Murphy Watson, Jacob B. Watson, Rolan Williams, and vacant land. The deed was signed by Arthur Watson and witnessed by John Frederick and Samuel Lewis. — On 12 June 1803 Thomas DeLoache sold 83 acres of this land to Shadrach Bailey. On 15 January 1810 he, then living in Lexington County, S.C., sold 116 acres to William Holston. On 25 March 1819 he sold 50 acres to Elizabeth Kirkland. — (Deed Book 23, page 2; Ibid. page 325; Ibid. 30, 1809-1811, page 85; Ibid. 35, 1818-1819, page 29.)

On 1 January 1806 Thomas DeLoache, then living in Lexington, S.C., bought from Job Padget 100 acres of land (part of an original grant to Job Padget) on Clouds Creek, bounding on Job Padget and Grigsbys Old Road. The deed was signed by Job Padget and witnessed by William DeLoache (then living in Lexington County) and Job Padget, Jr. — (Deed Book 27, page 442.)

On 5 March 1814 Thomas DeLoache bought from Jacob Dominick 204 acres of land (part of 820 acres granted to Daniel Cannon, Esqr.) on waters of Clouds Creek, lying on the road from Augusta to Columbia. The deed was signed by Jacob Dominick and witnessed by William DeLoache (then of Edgefield County) and Michael Kinard. — (Deed Book 32, page 405.)

In Lexington County, S.C.

On 9 November 1807, Thomas DeLoache, then living in Lexington County, sold (for the amount of $20.00) to John Quattlebaum 16 acres of land in Lexington County. — (Brent H. Holcombe - Memorialized Records of Lexington County, S.C., 1814-1825, pages 92 and 93.) At about 1809 (actually in 1807) John Quattlebaum moved from his home two miles north of the present town of Leesville (Lexington County), S.C., to a mill site on Lightwood Creek four miles south of Leesville. — (Paul Quattlebaum — Quattlebaum, a Palatine Family in South Carolina, page 7.) In view of this circumstance it appears that John Quattlebaum established his new home on the 16 acres of land which he bought from Thomas DeLoache, and that the said 16 acres were part of a larger tract acquired and lived on by Thomas DeLoache while he was a resident of Lexington County during the period of 1805-1814. Most of the records in Lexington County courthouse were burned during the War Between the States; therefore, nothing further is known concerning Thomas' land holdings in that county. In this connection it is noted that at the time of the 1840 census Thomas' son Allison DeLoache was living in Lexington County, and then was the owner of twenty slaves. — (Did Allison buy or inherit property which formerly was part of his father's estate?)

The above-mentioned transactions indicate that Thomas acquired at least a total of 674 acres of land in Edgefield County, of which he sold 299 acres and retained at least 374 acres until the time of his death.

On 22 June 1810, while living in Lexington County, Thomas DeLoache (preacher of the gospel and of the Baptist order) made his will in the following "manner and form", the witnesses thereto being Thomas Barkley, Mary Spencer, Joel Bell, and Shepard Spencer (Justice of the Peace).

"My will is that all my estate lands, goods and chattels, profits, debts, dues, demands and income shall remain in the hands of my beloved wife, Sarah, during her natural life or widowhood in order that she may thereby be enabled to school and educate my children but, and if my wife, Sarah, shall marry again then my wish is that all of my estate, real and personal, be sold on a credit of twelve months and the money arising from such sales to be divided in the following manner, to writ: To my eight eldest children, William DeLoache and Lucy Hunter and Cata Hunter, Thomas DeLoache and Elizabeth Bush and John DeLoache and Polly and Nancy, I give one dollar to each of them, and the rest of my estate to be equally divided amongst my wife, Sarah, and her children which she may have by me, my wife to have a child's part, but and if my wife, Sarah, shall decease without a second marriage, at her death, I leave my estate to be sold in the manner that is aforesaid described and divided amongst my children as aforesaid, that is, my eight oldest children to have one dollar each of them and the rest to be equally divided amongst my children which I have got by my last wife, Sarah. And I do nominate, constitute and appoint my said wife, Sarah, sole executrix of this my last will and testament . . . ."—— (The eight children of the first wife doubtless had previously received a portion of their father's estate, and the gift of one dollar each was to indicate that they had not been overlooked.)

On 4 October 1819 the will was proved in Edgefield County by Shepard Spencer; and on 18 October 1819, the second wife being then deceased, the third wife was appointed to act as executrix and "administer to the estate". An inventory (apparently a partial one) of the personal property of Thomas DeLoache, was returned on 6 November 1819. — (Edgefield County, S.C., Probate Records: File 8, Pack 296; Will Book C, page 34; Inventories, 1800-1820: — Book E, 1816-1820, page 442.) The probate records also include a sworn statement made on 20 December 1823 by Charity DeLoache (the third wife) as to correctness of the following items in the settlement account of Thomas' estate. She then was living in Butler County, Ala.

    a. Cash paid to William Ridlehoover.
    b. Purchasers at sale of the estate:
        Charity DeLoache (widow of the testator).
        William DeLoache (son of the testator).
        Mahala DeLoache (daughter of the testator).
        Sarah DeLoache (daughter of the testator).
        Thomas DeLoache (son of the testator).

From Thomas' will it is noted that he had a particular concern that his children be educated. At the time of the 1800 and 1810 censuses only his youngest children in each of these years were living in his home. The oldest children, except those who had died, evidently were attending school away from home and some of them married prior to 1810-1820.

The following information is known concerning the eight children named in Thomas' will and the nine children whose names are recorded in a family Bible owned by Mr. C.B. Smith (descendant of one of the daughters) who in 1940 was president of State Teachers College at Troy, Ala. Some of these children were born in the present Saluda County and others were born in Lexington County.

1. William (ca. 1780; lvg. 1840). — See previous mention of him in this sketch. In correspondence with certain persons during 1969-1972/3 this writer inadvertently identified him as a son of his uncle Michael Allison DeLoache (SKETCH No. 4a) who probably also had a son William.

At about 1800 William married Francis? Gossett, a daughter of John and Sarah Gossett. The 1800 census for Edgefield County shows him and his wife as sojourners in his father's home. On 10 November 1817 Sarah Gossett, widow, relinquished her right and claim of administration of her deceased husband's estate and letters of administration were granted to William DeLoache on 10 November 1817. At the time of the 1820 census she was living in William's home. — (Edgefield County, S.C., Probate Records: Box 11, Pack 381.) — In June 1805 he was a member of a committee which met at Mount Willing (in the present Saluda County) to draft a constitution for Sardis Baptist Church, which was constituted (organized) from Clouds Creek Baptist Church in June 1804. — (H.L. Baggott — History of Sardis Baptist Church, 1804-1904, page 2; Leah Townsend — South Carolina Baptists, 1670-1805, page 303.) — In the 1810-1830 censuses for Edgefield County he is listed as the head of a separate household, and in that county he bought and sold land — (Deed Book 32, page 211; Deed Book 34, page 119; Deed Book 35, page 461.) — In 1817 and again in 1821 he was appointed Justice of the Peace for Edgefield District. — (Laws of South Carolina — Acts of the Legislature, 1817 and 1821.) — At about 1835 he moved to Harris County, Ga., where some of his sons and their wives previously (on 8 September 1832) had become charter members of Bethany Baptist Church in that county. His wife died prior to the 1840 census for Harris County, and at the time of that census he was living with his son Augustus Wiles DeLoache.

William was the father of thirteen children whose names were learned from various records (including family records of some of his descendants). — SAMUEL was twice married (second wife was Catherine) and had issue. He lived variously in Monroe County, Ga. (1830), Harris County, Ga. (1832 - charter member of Bethany Baptist Church), Macon County, Ga. (1840), Barbour County, Ala. (1850), and Pike County, Ala. (1860). At the time of the 1820 census he was living with his grandfather's widow (Charity DeLoache) in Edgefield County, S.C., — THOMAS was twice married (wives were Julia Ann Elizabeth Martin? and Jane N. Cargil) and had issue. He lived variously in Monroe County, Ga. (1830), Harris County, Ga. (1832 - charter member of Bethany Baptist Church, and participated in the Land Lottery; listed in the 1840 census), Macon County, Ala. (1850), and Tallapoosa County, Ala. (1860).

At the time of the 1820 census he was living with his grandfather's widow (Charity DeLoache) in Edgefield County, S.C. — JOHN was twice married (wives were Elizabeth Sawyer and Rebecca _____) and had issue. He lived variously in Harris County, Ga. (1840), and Claiborne Parish, La. (1850 and 1860). — JAMES A. married and had issue. In 1832 he became a charter member of Bethany Baptist Church in Harris County, Ga., and was listed in the 1840 census for that county. In 1836-7 he was on the muster roll of the 67th Regiment, 2nd Division, from Harris County. — WILLIAM P. was twice married (wives were Mary Hickey and Frances _____) and had issue. In 1832 he and his wife Frances became charter members of Bethany Baptist Church in Harris County, Ga., and he participated in the Land Lottery. He was listed in the 1840 and 1850 censuses for that county. In 1836-7 he was on the muster roll of the 67th Regiment, 2nd Division, from Harris County. — ROBERT participated in the 1832 Land Lottery, being then a resident of Harris County, Ga. — AUGUSTUS WILES on 25 September 1833 became a member of Dry Creek Baptist Church in the present Saluda County, S.C. At about 1835 he moved to Harris County, Ga., where in 1837 he married Theodocia Spence by whom he had issue. He was listed in the 1840 and 1850 censuses for Harris County. His widow and children were listed in the 1860 census for Coosa County, Ala. In 1836 he (apparently as "Austin" DeLoach) was on the muster roll of the Georgia 6th Regiment. — NATHAN participated in the 1832 Land Lottery, being then a resident of Harris County, Ga. — MICHAEL ALBERT was twice married (wives were Charity Whittle and Mrs. Emeline, nee Haltiwanger, Rushton) and had issue. He lived variously in Harris County, Ga. (1832 - charter member of Bethany Baptist Church), Monroe County, Ga. (1840-listed in census for that year), Harris County, Ga. (1842 - bought land), and Edgefield County, S.C. (listed in the 1850 through 1890 censuses; acquired land in that part which is now Saluda County). He died in 1892 and was buried in Elmwood Cemetery at Ninety Six, S.C. — SON (apparently died in childhood). — DAUGHTER (Was she Elizabeth DeLoach who in 1843 married David Phelps in Harris County, Ga.?) — MARY married Thomas L. Grimmett of Merideth - Harris County, Ga. — DAUGHTER (Was she Jane DeLoach who in 1845 married James Gandy in Harris County, Ga.?)

2. Lucy (ca. 1781; lvg. 1810). — Prior to 1810 she married _____ Hunter.

3. Cata/Katie (ca. 1783; lvg. 1810) — Prior to 1810 she married _____ Hunter.

4. Thomas (22 October 1789; 25 November 1872). — In 1813 he married Sarah Bush (1797; 18 March 1877 — daughter of Isaac and Sarah/Sally Bush) and settled in Edgefield County, S.C., where he acquired land and lived the remainder of his life. He was listed in the 1820 through 1870 censuses for that county. In 1856 he was mentioned as Captain Thomas DeLoache. He and his wife are buried on the "DeLoache farm" near Harmony United Methodist Church. They were the parents of the following named fifteen children whose names are recorded in their family Bible. LEWELLYN (15 September 1814; lvg. 1860) married and had issue. — LAVINIA (14 October 1816; 15 May 1900) was twice married (husbands were Silas A.B. Villard and the Reverend Henry Dun-

ton). — NATHAN BUSH (14 October 1818; 3 June 1847). Unmarried. He was killed in the War with Mexico. His name is inscribed on a monument erected on the State House grounds in Columbia, S.C., — SARAH ANN (26 October 1820;   ) married Andrew Ramsey. — MARY CAROLINE (3 November 1822; 30 December 1886). Unmarried. — ELIZABETH AMANDA (23 October 1824; 19 November 1899) married Jarrett D. Burkhalter. — FRANCES EMALINE (23 June 1826; 14 October 1882). Unmarried. — LUCINDA ADELINE (21 September 1828,   ) married J. Bud Davis. — JOHN CALVIN (23 October 1830; killed in War Between the States). Unmarried. — THOMAS PRESTON (15 March 1833; 9 June 1878). Unmarried. — LUCRETIA (27 May 1835;   ) married Hudson Burkhalter. — JOSEPHINE (15 May 1837; died in infancy). — JABEZ MILLEGE (13 July 1839; 3 December 1911) married Catherine Warren and had issue. — CORDELIA JOSEPHINE (6 April 1841; 3 October 1883) married Milledge B. Ward. — WILLIAM MANLY (18 August 1844; 20 September 1914) married Emily E. _____ and had issue.

5. Elizabeth (ca. 1790; ca. 1818-20?). — In 1806-7 she married Herrin Bush, as his first wife, and had issue.

6. Polly (ca. 1792;   ) married a Mr. Brooks or a Mr. Williams.

7. John (ca. 1794; lvg. 1850). — At about 1818 he married Lucy Fluker (ca. 1798; lvg. 1850), who apparently was a daughter of Thomas Clement, the widow of Will Fluker, and the mother of three young daughters. He was a schoolteacher, and had moved from Edgefield (now Saluda) County, S.C., to central Georgia where he and Lucy were married. He lived variously in Clarke County, Ga. (1820), Perry County, Ala. (1830 and 1840), and Marengo County, Ala. (1850), being listed in the respective censuses for those counties. He and Lucy were the parents of seven children, two of whom (a son and a daughter) died in infancy or childhood. The surviving children were: — THOMAS CLEMENT (ca. 1819; lvg. 1860) married Mary S. Perryman and had issue. He was a practicing physician in Perry County, Ala. (1850) and in Marengo County, Ala. (1860). — MARIAH (ca. 1829; lvg. 1850). — WILLIAM L. (ca. 1831; lvg. 1860). He was a practicing physician in Marengo County, Ala. (1860). — JOHN (ca. 1834; lvg. 1850). — JAMES H. (ca. 1840; lvg. 1860).

8. Nancy (ca. 1796;   ) married a Mr. Williams or a Mr. Brooks.

9. Mahala (3 April 1804; ca. 1845-6). — At about 1828 she married William Ridlehoover (ca. 1795, ca. 1865), as his first wife, and became the mother of William, Jr., Joseph, Allison, Susan, Margaret and Julia Ridlehoover.

10. Sarah (15 August 1805; lvg. 1860). — At about 1828 she married John Henry Axson (7 July 1797; 7 March 1879) and became the mother of Robert Edward, Thomas, William A., John W., and Daughter (died in childhood) Axson.

Some data on the DeLoache-Axson family, apparently assembled by Mrs. Martha Ruth (Axson) Massie, was filed with the Caroliniana Library (at the University of South Carolina) in Columbia, S.C., prior to the year 1968. This data includes a copy (with many typing errors) of a letter sent by this writer to Mrs. Ralph L. Axson of St. Matthews, S.C., under date of 19 September 1948. On page 2 (paragraph 3) of this letter the name of "Samuel (who died 1760 in Edgecombe County, N.C.)", as had been given to this writer by a correspondent, was erroneously included as a son of William DeLoache, Jr.

The said data also includes a copy of a DeLoache record contained in THE HIGHLANDER, published by The Clan Campbell Association of America, 1937-1939. This record gives an erroneous origin of the DeLoache (DesLoges) family, and does not show its proper coat of arms. Furthermore, among other serious errors, the record contains a number of erroneous dates and wrongly shows the forementioned Samuel DeLoache as a son of William DeLoache, Jr.

11. Simeon (17 August 1807; 14 November 1822).

12. Floyd (10 September 1808; lvg. 17 March 1845). — He perhaps was the F.W. DeLoache listed in the 1840 census for Edgefield County, S.C., with a number of persons included in his household.

13. Allison (22 April 1810; 2 July 1887). — See SKETCH No. 6.

14. Madison (12 March 1812;   ). — No further information.

15. Marandia (14 October 1813; lvg. 1865). — In 1833 she married Jacob Sherwood Fannin (25 January 1811; 6 August 1881) at Mount Willing, S.C., and shortly thereafter they moved to Alabama. The 1860 census shows that they then were living in Coffee County, Ala. On one occasion her brother Allison DeLoache visited them in their Alabama home. Both of them died at Shady Grove (Pike County), Ala. They were the parents of thirteen children: — Mahaly Elizabeth, Lucretia Caroline, Daniel Herlong, John Broxon, Martha Maranda, Thomas DeLoach, Sarah Ann Wadkins, Mary Milburn, Tilithia Lucinda, James R. Abraham, Rebecca, Jacob Berton, and John Floyd Powell Fannin. — (Information concerning this family was furnished to this writer by Mr. C.B. Smith, a descendant, who in 1940 was president of State Teachers College at Troy, Ala. He then had in his possession an old Bible which belonged to his great-grandmother "Miranda" DeLoache Fannin. This Bible contained a record of the children of the Reverend Thomas DeLoache and his second wife, Sarah Watkins.)

16. Bainbridge (18 May 1816;   ). — No further information.

17. Lucretia (7 June 1818;   ). — No further information.

SKETCH No. 6
ALLISON DeLOACHE

Allison DeLoache (22 April 1810; 2 July 1887). — He was born in Lexington County, S.C., where his parents then were living. They took him with them on their return to Edgefield (now Saluda) County, S.C. He was eight years of age when his mother died and nine years of age when his father died. After their deaths he probably lived with his mother's parents (John Watkins and wife of Edgefield County ?). After his sister Sarah's marriage to John Henry Axson (in 1828) he lived in their home until about 1837, when he married Susannah Catherine Burton (9 January 1817; 29 September 1867) who was a daughter of Nathaniel and Susannah (Asbell) Burton of Edgefield County.

After their marriage Allison and Susannah settled in Lexington County, on lands which probably were formerly owned by his father, where the 1840 census lists him as the father of an infant son and the owner of twenty-four slaves. Prior to 1848 he returned to Edgefield County where he lived until the time of his death. He and his wife are buried in the cemetery at Red Bank Baptist Church in the present town of Saluda, S.C. He was an honored member and deacon of the said church.

The total of the land holdings of Allison DeLoache has not been determined by this writer. He doubtless owned the land on which he lived in Lexington County. The following listed real estate transactions engaged in by him are of record, as appropriate, either in the State Archives At Columbia, S.C., or in the courthouse at Edgefield, S.C.

Prior to 1848 Allison DeLoache and William Bouknight acquired 150 acres of land situated on waters of Mine Creek and bounded by lands of John Wingard, William Watkins, Jacob Pow, Jane Weaver, Jacob Pow, and Smith. On 3 January 1848 they sold this land to Ellen Crowder for $600.00 — (Deed Book HHH, page 302). It is assumed that Allison had a one-half interest in this land.

On 1 June 1852 Allison DeLoache was granted 364 acres of land situated in Edgefield District on the Canebrake Creek of Little Saluda River. — (Land grants, Vol. 88, page 20.) The grant was signed by His Excellency J.H. Means, Governor and Commander-in-Chief in and over the State of South Carolina. On 5 February 1885 Allison sold 300 acres of this land to his son Zebulon DeLoache for the amount of $100.00. This land then was described as adjoining lands of B.J. Bouknight, J.M. Forrest, Bailey Matthis, the said Allison DeLoache, and others. In the deed Allison stated: — "Now I the said Allison DeLoache do intend by this deed to give my son the said Zebulon DeLoache this advantage over the rest of my children. That is, the above specified tract of land being the home tract or the tract I now live on or so much of it as above specified to the said Zebulon DeLoache being crippled and not an able bodied man." — (Deed Book 8, page 487.)

On 14 October 1858 Allison DeLoache bought from Tillman H. Clark 100 acres of land which formerly belonged to Samuel Banks. This tract adjoined lands of Willis L. Stone, Mark Etheredge, R.R. Grigsby, and former land of James Rushton. At the same time he bought from Clark 19¼ acres of land formerly belonging to James Rushton. This tract adjoined lands of John Gillion, Rhydon Grigsby, and the said 100 acres.

The amount of $1,041.00 was paid for the two tracts as a whole. — (Deed Book JJJ, page 418.)

On 16 October 1866 Allison DeLoache bought from Z.W. Carwile (Commissioner of the Equity Court) 200 acres of land belonging to the estate of Willis L. Stone, Tract No. 4, adjoining lands of Mark Etheredge and others. The purchase price of the land was $1,030.00, and DeLoache gave bond to Carwile to insure payment. — (Deed Book MMM, pages 188 and 227.)

On 1 December 1876 Allison DeLoache bought from Stanmore B. Griffin and Richard G. Bonham 472 acres of land (formerly land of J. Robert Pow) situated on Dry Creek waters of Little Saluda River and bounded by lands of Mrs. Elizabeth Stone (widow of Willis L. Stone), George Bell, J.S. Pow, Thomas Whittle, and others. The purchase price of the land was $1,000.00 — (Deed Book TTT, page 616.) — On 14 January 1882 Allison sold the land to J. Robert Pow, the former owner. — (Deed Book 6, page 390.)

On 1 November 1879 Allison DeLoache bought from James Rushton 30 acres of "piney woods" land (known as the "Rushton Tract") bounding on the estate of Mark Etheredge and lands of James Rushton, Bailey Matthews, and Allison DeLoache. The purchase price of the land was $150.00. — (Deed Book 8, page 488.) By his will Allison gave his son Zebulon DeLoache limited use of this land, after which it was to be sold and the proceeds to be equally divided among his (Allison's) heirs.

On a date and in a manner not yet determined Allison DeLoache acquired 217 acres of "piney woods" land known as the "Watkins Place". After his death this land was to be sold and the proceeds to be equally divided among his (Allison's) heirs. — (Deed Book F, page 641 — Will of Allison DeLoache.)

The following listed sales of land by Allison DeLoache, in addition to those heretofore mentioned, are of record in the courthouse at Edgefield.

On 1 January 1873 Allison DeLoache sold to Bailey Matthews 76 acres of land bounding on lands of Allison DeLoache, Mrs. Mary Bouknight, Bailey Crouch, and J.W. Edwards. — (Deed Book 4, page 41.)

On 11 September 1873 Allison DeLoache sold to Thomas Whittle 128½ acres of land bounding on lands of Mark Etheredge, Elizabeth Stone, John Gillion, and Thomas Whittle. The sale price of the land was $1,000.00. — (Deed Book 2, page 245.)

From the foregoing it will be noted that in the aggregate over a period of years Allison acquired at least 1,477¼ acres of land in Edgefield (now Saluda) County, S.C. At the time of his death he owned none of this except the 247 acres mentioned in his will. During his lifetime he disposed of 1,230¼ acres, of which 1,051½ acres were disposed of by known deeds of sale; but such deeds for the remaining 178¾ acres were not found in the records searched by this writer. At the time of the 1860 census for Edgefield County the value of his real estate and personal property was reported as $17,250.00. In addition to being a planter, for a number of years he operated a country store on his home plantation. As heretofore mentioned, the major portion of this plantation (with all buildings (including the store building) was sold to his son Zebulon DeLoache, with whom he lived until the time of his death.

On 6 March 1854 Allison DeLoache and James Spann witnessed the will of Margaret A. Pow of Edgefield (now Saluda) County, S.C.

Allison DeLoache is listed in the 1840 census for Lexington County and in the 1850 through 1880 censuses for Edgefield county. The names of all his children, except one who died when about three months of age, are shown in these censuses and some of them are mentioned in his will.

Will of Allison DeLoache, dated 28 April 1887 and probated 10 August 1887. — (Mobley Township) — I give to my daughter-in-law Mary DeLoache my entire possession of household and kitchen furniture; also one note I hold against Zebulon DeLoache for $471.00, dated 19 January 1881, with interest that may accrue thereon. I give to my son Zebulon DeLoache the entire use of my piney woods tract of land known as the Rushton Tract (about 30 acres) to have and to hold until the youngest child of James N. DeLoache and Mary Carson shall arrive at the age of 21, after which the said 30 acres reverts to my estate. I direct that my piney woods tract known as the Watkins Place be rented, leased, or used to the best advantage for the heirs, which contain about Two Hundred and 17 acres, until the said minor heirs of James N. DeLoache and Mary Carson shall have arrived at the age of 21, after which I direct that my executor put and sell to the highest bidder the above mentioned tract of land including the said 30 acres of land and that the proceeds be equally divided among my heirs . . . The residue and remainder of my estate I order and direct both real and personal to be sold as soon after my death as my executor sees proper and fit and the proceeds to be equally divided among my heirs.

And lastly I do hereby appoint and nominate my son-in-law
Josh W. Edwards Executor . . . Witnesses: Baily Matthews,
J.F. Kirkland, James M. Forrest.

A settlement account (evidently a partial settlement) on Allison's estate and the original of his will are contained in File 116, Pack 4723, in the office of the Probate Judge at Edgefield Courthouse. This account shows that payments were made to his sons-in-law in right of their wives.

Dr. L.B. Bouchelle	$ 500.00
W.W. Holston	500.00
Rev. J.A. Carson	1,000.00*
J.W. Edwards	500.00
Dr. J.G.J. Davis	500.00

* He married two of Allison's daughters.

Allison and his wife Susannah were the parents of the ten following named children. Some of them were born in Lexington County and all others were born in the present Saluda County.

1. Wilson (16 September 1838; 16 September 1854). — He is buried in the cemetery at Red Bank Baptist Church.

2. Sarah/Sallie S. (ca. 1840; lvg. 1930) — In 1859 she was in charge of Spring Field Academy (near Mount Tabor Church in Edgefield County, where she taught ancient history and mental and practical arithmetic. On 20 December 1859 she married Dr. Lewis B. Bouchelle, who also was a schoolteacher. At the time of the 1860 census they were living in the home of Jacob and Nancy Wright at Fruit Hill in the present Saluda County. In 1930 she was living at Tennille, Ga. She and her husband were the parents of: — Susan (married Henry Wight. In 1948 they were living in Falls Church, Va.), Sophia (unmarried), Fred (married and lived

39

in West Virginia).

3. Elvira/Ellie (27 February 1843; 9 August 1915). — At about 1866-7 she married Joshua Walter Edwards (3 January 1843; 28 April 1910) and they settled on lands in the present Saluda County, S.C. He was the executor of the will of his father-in-law, Allison DeLoache. "Josh" and Ellie were members of Red Bank Baptist Church, and they are buried in the cemetery at that church. They were the parents of: — Wilson Clark (married Laura Lawton Meredith and had issue), an unnamed son and an unnamed daughter who died in infancy, John Broadus (married Annie Belle Kenney and had issue), Robert Lee (died in infancy), William Allison (married Jessie Lane and had issue), Susan (married John Black; no issue), J. Bee (died in infancy), and Elizabeth/Bess (lvg. in 1981, over 99 years of age and the last surviving member of her immediate family; unmarried).

4. Louisa/Lou (ca. 1845; ca. 1916). — At about 1867-8 she married Woodruff Wilson Holstein (ca. 1844;   ) and they settled on lands in the present Saluda County, S.C. "Woody" and Lou were members of West Creek Baptist Church in Saluda County. They were the parents of: — Mae (died unmarried), Sarah/Sallie (married John Wise and had issue), Geulah E. (died unmarried), Maud (died unmarried), James Connor (married Mamie Bodie; no issue), Webster/Webb B. (married Mamie Smith and had issue), and David Woodruff (died in the Spanish-American War; unmarried).

5. Zebulon/Zeb (23 October 1847; 17 September 1934). — See SKETCH No. 7.

6. Sophia/Soph (1850; 16 January 1930). — During a period of about thirty years she was a schoolteacher in the present Saluda County, S.C., and was the organizer of the first "Bond of Mercy" group in the state. Following her teaching career, and after graduating from medical colleges when it was difficult for a woman to enter the practice of medicine, she became the city physician in Augusta, Ga. She married Dr. John/Jack G.J. Davis, and together they practiced medicine in Augusta until the time of his death. After continuing her practice for a period of time she retired therefrom and organized in Augusta a humane society for the prevention of cruelty to animals, and ardently served many years as its president and later as a field worker. She and her husband are buried in a cemetery at Tennille, Ga. A lengthy tribute to her was published in the Augusta Herald and republished in an issue of the Saluda Standard. She was the mother of Sophia Carrie Davis, an adopted daughter.

7. James Nathaniel (30 August 1852; 12 July 1879). — He died by drowning in Little Saluda River, in Saluda County, S.C. At about 1873 he married Elizabeth/Lizzie E. Edwards (11 June 1846; 18 March 1908). Both of them are buried in the cemetery at Red Bank Baptist Church. They were the parents of: — JULIA (ca. 1874;   ) married Mr. Woodward. — SUSANNA A. (28 May 1875; 20 January 1950) married Daniel P. Norris (12 October 1871; 5 December 1952) and had issue. Both of them are buried in the cemetery at Red Bank Baptist Church. — JAMES ALLISON (ca. 1878; 31 August 1961) married Emma Gregory, and they were the parents of: — Clyde E., Allison, Harry Bell, and four daughters (Mrs. Jimmie Spurlin, Mrs. D.D. Johnson, Mrs. J.L. Temple, and Mrs. Earl Leopard), all of whom were living in 1961.

8. Mary (15 September 1854;   June 1879). — At about 1875 she married the Reverend James A. Carson (1850; 1929) as his first wife, and they were the parents of: — Benjamin Franklin (1876-1968) married Mattie Sloan and had issue. — James Allison (1879-   ) married Maude Parrish and had issue. The Reverend James A. Carson and his son Benjamin Franklin Carson both were Baptist preachers.

9. Josephine L. (23 August 1858; 8 May 1903). — At about 1881 she married the Reverend James A. Carson (1850; 1929) as his second wife, and they were the parents of: Ora Allein (1882;   ) married Bob Crawford and had issue. — William Burton (1886;   ) married and had issue. — Andrew Boyce (1889;   ) married Anne Rutledge and had issue. — Leta Elvira (1891;   ) married Guy Forrest and had issue. — William Edwin (1895;   ) married Fern Christian and had issue. — Louis Frederick (1897;   ) married Mae Jones and had issue. — A child who died in childhood. The Reverend Mr. Carson and his two wives are buried in the cemetery at Red Bank Baptist Church.

ASBILL

This family name appears in various records under different forms of spelling, such as: — Asbald, Asball, Asbel, Asbell, Asbil, Asbill, Asble, Aspull, and Azbell.

According to the Magazine of American Genealogy, No. 8 (March 1930), p. 80, and No. 9 (April 1930), p. 81, — (with reference to Green's "Early Virginia Immigrants", 1623-1666, pages 13 and 14), — in 1641 one George Ashall (Asball) was brought to Virginia by Ambrose Bennett; and in 1650 one George Asball was brought to Virginia by Robert Bird. It is speculated that the one who came first was a son of the one who came last. It is said that these men came from Devonshire (County Devon), England, and that there were three brothers in the family, namely: — George, Richard, and Adam (mentioned as Adam Aspull). In 1652 George Asball (evidently the younger one) was given a grant of 350 acres of land in Virginia. — (Handbook of American Genealogy, Vol. 47.)

George Asball (ca. 1610; 1672), one of three brothers, married Mary Fowler? and settled in Lower Norfolk (later Nansemond) County, Va. On 1 September 1671 he made his will (proved on 16 February 1672) in which he described himself as "George Asball of Ye Little Creek in Linhaven Parish, Lower Norfolk County, Virginia". By this will he gave to his wife Mary the home plantation to enjoy during her life, but it was to become the property of his son George when he arrived at the age of 16 years. — To his older son Richard (see following) he gave the plantation called Wolves Neck (probably the forementioned 350 acres of land) and other property. To his daughters Elizabeth, Mary, and Susannah he gave certain property. His wife was named as executor, and his friend George Fowler (probably a brother-in-law, sometimes called friend when named in a will) was named as overseer. — (Brief abstracts of Lower Norfolk County, Va., Wills, — Book E, p. 134.)

Richard Asball (ca. 1633; 1700), son of George and Mary Asball, was born in Devonshire, England. At about 1655 he married Anne Markes,

41

Allison DeLoache

Susannah Catherine Burton
(wife of Allison DeLoache)

daughter of Peter Markes of Lower Norfolk County, Va., who was the mother of Asball children among whom were Elizabeth (married William Charlton) and Anne (married William Privett). Richard, his wife (Anne), and Elizabeth are named in the will (dated 19 August 1656 and proved on 15 October 1656) of Peter Markes, and Richard was named as sole executor of the will. — (Brief Abstracts of Lower Norfolk County, Va., Wills, — Book D, p. 10.) —— After the death of Anne (his wife), Richard married Mary Martin (living in 1795) who was the mother of Asball children among whom were Martin (see following) and Mary. Prior to 1695 he moved to Chowan County, N.C., where he died leaving a will (dated 15 September 1695). The will mentions his wife (Mary), daughter Mary, and a child in esse, all of my children (including the husbands of his daughters Elizabeth and Anne). The will is of record in the Chowan County Courthouse. — (North Carolina Genealogical and Historical Register, Vol. 1, p. 26.)

Martin Asball (ca. 1680; lvg. 1742), son of Richard and Mary Asball, probably was born in Chowan County, N.C. At about 1704 he married Hannah Pierce, daughter of John and Mary Pierce, and settled in Perquimans (formerly Berkeley) County, N.C., where he acquired land and where he probably died. It is said that on 13 April 1730 he made a will, but the time and place at which it was proved have not been determined by this writer. Among his children were Pierce (see following), Richard, Jean (in 1736 her father gave her lands in Perquimans County), Margaret (born 13 September 1717), and Ann (born 18 July 1734). In addition to giving lands to his children he sold lands to other persons. — (North Carolina Historical and Genealogical Register, Vol. 3, p. 379.)

Pierce Asball (ca. 1705;   ), son of Martin and Hannah Asball, was born in Perquimans County, N.C. On 3 January 1742 his father gave him a plantation in that county, the disposition of which has not been learned by this writer. He moved to Orange County in the Hillsboro District of North Carolina, where he acquired land. Orange County, formed in 1752, originally embraced the area included in its five present-day adjoining counties and parts of six farther removed counties. The exact location of Pierce's residence has not been determined. In the Orange County records his given name is shown as Pierce or Pearce, and his surname is written in various forms of spelling. The name of his wife, the total number of his children, and the time and place of his death have not been learned. Donald Eugene Bennett and George T. Bennett, pages 28 and 29 of their record of "The Asbill Family", mention authentic records which show the names of four sons: — John (married Elizabeth Cornelius), Joseph, James (married _____ Whitnum?), and Solomon. The finding of this writer concerning these four men, which in regard to Joseph does not agree with the record of the Messrs. Bennett, is stated in the following paragraphs.

1. John. — He married Elizabeth Cornelius and settled in Chowan County, where his will (dated 29 July 1796) was proved at the December 1796 term of court. Among his six children he mentions a son Cornelius (his wife's maiden name). — (Olds. — Abstract of North Carolina Wills, 1760-1800, p. 61; North Carolina Historical and Genealogical Register, Vol. 1, p. 516.)

2. Joseph. — See following.

3. James. — He married _____ Whitnum and settled in Bertie County, N.C., where he is included in the 1790 census.

4. Solomon (died in 1769). — He died in Bertie County, N.C., and at the court term of 1769 his twin sons Joseph and Solomon, aged six years, were committed to the tuition of Malachi Frazier. — (North Carolina Genealogical and Historical Register, Vol. 3, p. 447.) —— Joseph married Fanny _____ and settled in Bertie County, where he is included in the 1790 census and where he died in 1827 leaving a will (dated 19 October 1826 and proved at the court term of February 1827. - (Ibid., Vol. 2, p. 498.) The Messrs. Bennett erroneously identify him as the Joseph Asball who married Dorthy Ross. —— Solomon (Jr.) married (1) Sarah Jernigan on 25 August 1784; and (2) Elizabeth _____ who is named in his will (dated 1 November 1849 and proved at the court term of February 1850). — (Ibid., Vol. 2, pp. 218 and 498.) He supposedly was living in the home of some other person in Bertie County at the time of the 1790 census.

Joseph Asball (ca. 1735; lvg. 1790), son of Pierce and Hannah Asball, was born in Perquimans County, N.C. During 1761 he served in the French and Indian War. On 30 May 1778, in Lenoir County, N.C., he took an oath of allegiance to defend the State of North Carolina against King George the Third. He served as an inspector to check the loyalty of North Carolina officials to the American cause. — (North Carolina State Records, Vol. 22, p. 172.) He was listed in the 1790 census for Pitt County, N.C., — which adjoins Lenoir County, — where he probably settled prior to or during 1778. At about 1757 he married Dorothy Ross (died before 1790?), daughter of the Reverend George Aeneas Ross (1676; 1754) who is said to have been a descendant of Mac-an-t-Sagairt (created Earl of Ross in 1234) of Scotland. The Reverend Mr. Ross, who was educated at the University of Edinburgh and served both as a Presbyterian minister and an Episcopalian minister, came to America in 1700 and settled at New Castle, Delaware. It is not stated how, when, or where Dorothy Ross met Joseph Asball, but after their marriage she went with him to North Carolina. Their children are said to have been: — Aaron (see following), William (married 1. Malinda Ross and 2. Elizabeth Moore), James (married, 1782, Pauline Coyle), John (married, 1788, Elizabeth Coyle), Elizabeth (married, 1792, Zadock Piercy), Nannie (married, 1797, William Mitchell), and three sons (names not given) included in the 1790 census for Pitt County.

Aaron Asball (ca. 1758; 1814), said to be a son of Joseph and Dorothy Asball, probably was born in Perquimans County, N.C. Among his descendants were Pierce Belton Asball, Joseph Burton, and Dorothy Burton, the last two being children of Nathaniel Burton who married 1. Aaron's daughter Susannah and 2. Edea Whittle. The given names (Pierce, Joseph, and Dorothy) of these descendants are a strong indication of Aaron's parentage. At about 1778 he married Ann/Nancy _____ (born about 1760; died after 1814) who might have been a Miss Belcher, or a Miss Jarvis who named one of her sons Jarvis Asball. He settled in Bertie County, N.C., where he bought and sold land, and was included in the 1790 census for that county. The last sale of land was made in 1799, and soon thereafter he moved to Edgefield County, S.C., where he was included in the 1800 census. ——

In the new location he settled near Ridge Spring, which now is in the present Saluda County, S.C. He acquired several hundred acres of land, most of which eventually became the possession of three of his sons. A tract of 267 acres (the plantation on which he last resided) was acquired by his son Jarvis Asball on 3 September 1814 following his father's death. The settlement papers on Aaron's estate, together with other records, mention his wife Ann and show the names of his sons and their wives and his daughters and their husbands, as follows: —

    1. Nancy (born ca. 1779). — Married Josiah Todd.

    2. John (born ca. 1780). — Married Abigail Frederick.

    3. Penelope (born ca. 1782). — Married Charles Williamson.

    4. Susannah (11 June 1784; 23 August 1841). — Married Nathaniel Burton.

    5. Lewis (born ca. 1786). — Married Mary/Polly Satcher.

    6. Elisha (born ca. 1788). — Married A. _____.

    7. Jarvis (born ca. 1790). — Married Frances Deshazo.

    8. Hepsibah/Hepsy (born ca. 1792) — Married John/E.W. Browning.

In South Carolina the family name now is spelled "Asbill".

BURTON

The name of this family is of English derivation, and is by origin a place name signifying **burgtun** or **boroughtown**. It has been variously spelled as Bearden, Berden, Burden, Burdine, Burtin, and Burton.

During the reign (1625-1649) of King Charles the First two Burton brothers, Thomas (see following) and John, came from England to Virginia and settled in that part of old Henrico County which later became Chesterfield County. It is said of these brothers and their descendants in Virginia: — "Among all the families of which the memory is preserved, it would be difficult to match the Burtons of Henrico County for lack of the romantic. They were a most respectable lot, devoting their lives for one generation after another to getting lands, getting children, and growing tobacco." — (Francis Burton Harrison — Burton Chronicles of Colonial Virginia.)

Thomas Burton (ca. 1630-4; 1686), the immigrant, acquired and disposed of land in Henrico County, Va. Shortly before his death he gave some of this land to his four sons. — (Henrico County, Va., Record Book I, p. 350.) At about 1655 he married Susannah (believed to have been the daughter of Abraham Wood), who administered his estate and later married John Stewart. She was the mother of the said four sons, — Thomas, John (see following), Isaac, and Abraham, — and perhaps other Burton children. Abraham Wood was born in 1610 and died in 1684 (?).

John Burton (1666; 1754). — The year of his birth is shown by a deposition made by him on 12 October 1688. — (Henrico County, Va., Record Book V, p. 11.) His stepfather, John Stewart, was his legal guardian for about one year. He became of age in 1687, and then took over the land which his father had given to him and engaged in farming and merchandising. He was a large tobacco grower. During the period of 1701-1720 he acquired an additional 1,480 acres plus a plantation (acreage not stated in reference) which he leased from Thomas Jefferson and eventually bought. — (Record Books of Henrico County, Va.; Francis Burton Harrison — Burton Chronicles of Colonial Virginia.)

At about 1687-8 he married Elizabeth Fowler (ca. 1671; 1757), daughter of Samuel Fowler, Sr., who mentions her in his will (made in 1688). Her will, probated in 1757, is recorded in Chesterfield County, Va., Will Book 1, page 314. His will, dated 23 February 1754, is recorded in Chesterfield County, Va., Will Book 1, page 208. They were the parents of: — A daughter (married William Shepherd; died before 1754), — John (married Elizabeth _____; died in 1747; his son Robert Burton was in South Carolina on 20 January 1752, and was included in the 1790 census for Edgefield County, S.C.), — Thomas (married Joanna _____; died in 1773), — Samuel, — James (married Judith _____; died in 1783), — Sarah (married _____ Jackson), — Elizabeth (made will in 1767; married _____ Turpin), — Susannah (married _____ Tanner), — Febue/Phoebe (married _____ Johnson), — Ann (married, about 1755, Charles? Pain), — Esar/Isaiah (see following), — Robert (married _____ Ward?).

Isaiah Burton (ca. 1707; lvg. 1763) was born in Henrico (later Chesterfield) County, Va. In 1728, when he was 21 years of age and apparently at about the time of his marriage, his father deeded to him 85 acres of land in that county. — (Henrico County, Va., Deeds and Wills, 1725-1737, p. 256.) He married Obedience _____, who was living in 1753 when she brought suit against one Charles Burton of Chesterfield County. In 1736 Isaiah bought 600 acres of land in Henrico County from Henry Cary. A county court order issued in February 1745 shows that Isaiah Burton, his son Isaiah Burton, Jr. (born before or during 1729), and other persons were named to assist John Branch in surveying a road. In 1751 he deeded to John Fowler the forementioned 600 acres of land, which then were lying in Chesterfield County, and Obedience Burton (his wife) relinquished her dower rights. Nathaniel Burton (believed to be Isaiah's son) was one of the witnesses. — (Chesterfield County, Va., Deed Book 1, p. 252.)

At some time between 1753 and 1757 Isaiah Burton moved to Albemarle County, Va., where in the latter year he deeded the forementioned 85 acres of land in the then Chesterfield County to Abraham Cowley. — (Chesterfield County, Va., Deed Book III, p. 129.) On the same day in 1757 he bought from Ware Rockett of New Kent County, Va., 200 acres of land (part of 1,500 acres which belonged to his brother Thomas Burton) in Chesterfield County. — (Chesterfield County, Va., Deed Book III, p. 120.).

The next record found of Isaiah Burton, Sr., places him in Buckingham (adjoining Albemarle) County, Va., where in 1763 he deeded the forementioned 200 acres of land in Chesterfield County to his nephew John Burton. One of the witnesses was William Burton (believed to be Isaiah's son). — (Chesterfield County, Va., Deed Book IV., p. 456.) The records of Buckingham County have not been searched for further information concerning him. It is said that there is no will recorded for him in that county; however, nothing is said of a possible administration on his estate, if he died intestate in Buckingham County.

In the "Burton Chronicles of Colonial Virginia", from which most of the preceding data was obtained, no mention is made of any lands which Isaiah Burton might have acquired while he lived in Albemarle and Buckingham Counties. The lands which he owned in Henrico/Chesterfield County were sold to persons who were not members of his family, and he apparently (so far as the known records show) gave nothing to his children. The total number of his children is not known. Isaiah, Jr. (see following) is the only son who is definitely known. As heretofore stated, it is believed that Nathaniel and William were two other sons.

Isaiah Burton, Jr. (ca. 1729; 1775) was born in Henrico (later Chesterfield) County, Va. In 1745 he, then being a tithable (a male of sixteen years or over), was ordered to assist John Branch in surveying a road in the said county. Though this writer has not searched for further information concerning him in Virginia, it is believed that he was the Isaiah Burton who came from Virginia to South Carolina with his wife and children shortly before or during 1769.

After his arrival in the new location Isaiah Burton presented the following petitions to the Colonial Council of South Carolina for grants of land.

(a) Based on his previous petition, on 14 March 1769 a plat for 200 acres of land situated on Mudlick Creek in Berkley (now Newberry) County was certified for him, and the grant for the land was signed on 19 June 1772. — (Grant Book 26, p. 26.)

(b) On 3 April 1770 the Council approved his petition for another 200 acres of land in the same county, but the grant therefor lapsed due to his failure to take up the land. On 7 January 1772 the Council approved his petition to certify the lapsed grant.

(c) On 4 December 1770 the Council approved his petition for 200 acres of land in Craven (now Newberry) County.

The petitions of Isaiah Burton for a total of 600 acres of land indicate that eleven persons (himself, presumably his wife, and nine children) were included in his family when he arrived in South Carolina. He was allowed 100 acres for himself and 50 acres for each other person. Apparently no grants for items (b) and (c) were issued in his name, and it is probable that he sold the warrants for the land to other persons who received the grants. Newberry County formerly was part of old Craven County, part of which lay north of Saluda River. In a number of instances the petitions, plats, and grants show Berkley County, which lay south of Saluda River, whereas the land actually was in Craven County.

On 7 March 1775 a dedimus was issued to Robert Cunningham, Esqr. (then of Craven County), to prove the will of Isaiah Burton, deceased, and to qualify the executors therein named. — (Brent H. Holcomb — Probate Records of South Carolina, Vol. 2, p. 150.) This writer made a fruitless effort to find the will, which probably was destroyed during the Revolutionary War period. No record known to this writer shows the number and names of Isaiah's children; however, one of his sons evidently was the Nathan Burdine/Nathaniel Burton (see following) included in the 1790 census for Newberry County, S.C.

Nathan Burdine/Nathaniel Burton (born about 1753; lvg. 1790) came with his father to Newberry County, S.C., prior to or during 1769. One of his grandsons, then an aged man, stated that his grandfather was an American soldier during the Revolutionary War; however, as in many other cases, the record of his service has been lost or destroyed. At the time of the 1790 census for Newberry County he was the head of a family consisting of himself, three other males, and seven females. The second son in the family was Nathaniel Burton, Jr. (see following). The names of the other children have not been learned by this writer.

Nathaniel Burton, Jr. (15 March 1778; 5 July 1865) was born in Newberry County, S.C. At about 1800 he moved to Edgefield County, S.C., and married Susannah Asbill (11 June 1784; 23 August 1841), daugher of Aaron Asbill (which see). He acquired land near the present town of Monetta (now in Saluda County), S.C., where he established a home and lived during the remainder of his life. He was a successful farmer, and the owner of a number of slaves. He was included in the 1800-1860 censuses for Edgefield County. He was a captain during the War of 1812, and he is mentioned as Captain Nathaniel Burton in his will. On 20 December 1842 he married Edea/Edie Whittle (10 October 1812; 22 December 1885) who, then a widow, was included in the 1870 and 1880 censuses for Edgefield County. At the time of the 1800 census a female of 26 to 45 years of age and three males under 10 years of age were living with him. It is believed that these were a widowed sister and her children. He married Susannah later in that year. Nathaniel Burton, his two wives, and some of his children were buried in marked graves in the family cemetery on his plantation near Monetta.

From family Bible records, tombstone inscriptions, and his will and estate papers (filed in the office of the Probate Judge at Edgefield, S.C.), it is known that Nathaniel Burton, Jr., was the father of eleven children by his first wife and two children by his second wife, these being: —

1. Penelope (ca. 1801; lvg. 1865). — Md. Gibeon J. Williams.
2. Nancy (ca. 1803; lvg. 1865). — Md. _____ Reynolds.
3. Dorothy (ca. 1805; lvg. 1865). — Md. Wiley Reynolds.
4. Isaiah (ca. 1806; lvg. 1865). — Md. Margaret Charity Mims.
5. Julia (ca. 1808; June 1815).
6. Washington (24 October 1810; 2 September 1831). — Unmarried.
7. Eleanor/Ellin (17 April 1812; 26 September 1839). — Md. Wade Holstein.
8. Nathaniel (1 January 1814; 3 June 1848). — Md. Sophia Connecticut Woodruff.
9. John (10 January 1816; 31 January 1857). — Unmarried.
10. Susannah (9 January 1817; 29 September 1867). — Md. Allison DeLoache (which see).
11. Edna (15 March 1820; 30 August 1841). — Unmarried.
12. James Benjamin (17 August 1844; bef. 1850).
13. Whit Joseph (29 October 1845; 2 April 1929). — Md. Mary S. Bodie.

SKETCH No. 7
ZEBULON DeLOACHE

Zebulon DeLoache (23 October 1847; 17 September 1934). — He probably was born in Edgefield (now Saluda) County, S.C. When about five or six years of age he was carried by his parents to the home which his father established on the place which had been granted to him in 1852. Other than during those times when he was attending school away from home, he lived with his parents during the remainder of their lives. As heretofore mentioned, on 5 February 1885 his father sold to him this homestead inclusive of 300 acres of land. He and his family are listed in the 1880 census for Edgefield County.

He was a studious and well-read person, having received a good education at the schools and academies which he attended. During a period of time he studied for the practice of medicine but, being of a very sensitive nature, he discontinued the study after having observed procedures in the operating room of the medical college which he was attending. He subsequently was employed as teacher at Pine Grove School in Edgefield (now Saluda) County and, together with his father, operated a country store situated near the home site. After his father's death he carried on farming operations with the help of hired hands and sharecroppers. He was not an able-bodied man, having been crippled by a fall from his nurse's arms during his infancy.

In the fall of 1898 Zebulon moved from his farm to Leesville, S.C., so that his children might have the benefit of the schools and college in that town. He or his son made regular visits to the farm to check on operations carried on there. In 1900/1 he traded a tract of 272 acres of land (situated in Orangeburg County, S.C., and bought by him in 1880) to David B. Busby for 40 acres of land and a commodious house built thereon. Mr. Busby formerly was the principle of Emory High School (sometimes called "College"), — a chartered institution having authority to grant to its graduates diplomas and the Bachelor of Arts degree, — which was situated about one air mile distance from Zebulon's farm. The house had been built by Mr. Busby as a residence for himself and as a dormitory for boarding students at the "college" which was nearby. After living in this house for a period of three or four years Zebulon sold the property (house and forty acres of land) to Walter J. Padgett and returned to his original home where he continued to live until his death in 1934.

At an early age he became a devout and dedicated Christian. In 1865, at the age of eighteen years, he united with the membership of Red Bank Baptist Church in the present town of Saluda, S.C. Taking turns with ministers who were present on such occasions, he preached in the annual "protracted" services which were held at the church. In 1870 he was licensed as a local preacher in the church; but, both by word of mouth and exemplary living, he imparted a Christian message to others without regard of denominational lines. His home was one in which the family alter held first place. Part of his daily routine was devoted to Bible reading and study, prayer, spiritual meditation, and the singing of religious songs. The joy of the Christian religion was truly manifested in his daily life, and this joy he always sought to share with others. The following are some of the many tributes paid to him after his decease.

"He was one of Saluda County's most beloved and God-fearing citizens." — "One could look the country over and not find a more devout Christian and God-fearing man." — "The glowing example of his life will live long in the lives and hearts of those who knew him and ever fondly admired him." — "He was a man whose almost every conversation led to things eternal." — "Many of us remember his earnest prayer, —somehow a sincerity, a power unusual."

On 8 February 1876 Zebulon married Mary Alice Matheny (24 October 1852; 10 August 1892), daughter of Charles R. and Eleanor J. (Wright) Matheny. Both of them are buried in the cemetery at Red Bank Baptist Church. They were the parents of the following named children.

1. Ellen (26 November 1876; 2 August 1948). — In addition to attending the forementioned Emory High School, she was a student at Johnston Academy (Johnston, S.C.) and Leesville College (Leesville, S.C.). On 2 November 1899 she married Henry Asbury Spann (ca. 1874; 1916), and on 22 December 1918 she married Benjamin James Padget (18 September 1875; 29 February 1920) as his second wife. She had no children. She is buried in the cemetery at Red Bank Baptist Church.

2. Alice (30 March 1878; 10 August 1903). — In addition to attending the forementioned Emory High School, she was a student at Johnston Academy (Johnston, S.C.) and Leesville College (Leesville, S.C.). She taught school, in Saluda and Orangeburg Counties, S.C., during a number of years before her death. She died unmarried, being buried in the cemetery at Red Bank Baptist Church.

3. James/Jim Nathaniel (28 October 1879; 5 October 1967). — See SKETCH No. 8.

4. Dora (3 December 1881; 5 March 1966). — In addition to attending the forementioned Emory High School, she was a student at Monetta Academy (Monetta, S.C.) and at an educational institution in Leesville, S.C. She taught school in Saluda County, S.C., during a number of years before her marriage. On 11 July 1911 she married Van Everett Edwards, as his second wife, and they lived the whole of their married lives in Johnston, S.C. Both of them are buried in Mount of Olives Cemetery in that town. They were the parents of: Mary Alice (married Eugene C. Mathis and had issue), Helen (married Frank W. Herlong and had issue), and Van Everett, Jr. (married 1st Alice White and 2nd Mary Gavin and had issue).

5. Mary (5 August 1883; 21 October 1961). — In addition to attending the forementioned Emory High School, she was a student at Monetta Academy (Monetta, S.C.) and at an educational institution in Leesville, S.C. She taught schools in Saluda, Greenwood, and Abbeville Counties, S.C., during a number of years before her marriage. For a period of two years between 1910 and 1913 she served as deaconess with a Methodist Church in Chester, S.C. On 7 June 1916 she married the Reverend Lewis Hill Smith, and they lived in Greenwood, S.C. during the last years of their married life. Both of them are buried in the cemetery at Friendship Pentecostal Holiness Church in Greenwood County. They were the parents of: — Mary Ruth (married Arthur Timmerman and had issue),

Lewis Hill, Jr. (married Ann Mercer and had issue), Rebecca (married Benjamin Garvin and had issue), and Zebulon DeLoache (married Rowena Stewart and had issue).

6. Susan (20 March 1885; 25 December 1972). — In addition to attending the forementioned Emory High School, she was a student at Monetta Academy (Monetta, S.C.) and at an educational institution in Leesville, S.C. During a period of twenty or more years she taught schools in Saluda County, S.C. On 15 September 1917 she married George Washington McCarty, and they lived in Saluda County during all of their married life. Both of them are buried in the cemetery at Butler United Methodist Church in that county. They were the parents of: — Dorothy Irene (married Maxwell Earle Stone and had issue).

7. Daniel (10 April 1888; 2 May 1888). — He is buried in the cemetery at Red Bank Baptist Church.

8. Sarah/Sallie (30 March 1889; 1 July 1959). — In addition to attending Leesville Elementary School in Leesville, S.C., Pine Grove Elementary School and Emory Graded School in Saluda County, S.C., she was a student at Saluda High School in the town of Saluda. She subsequently was enrolled as a student in Summerland College near Batesburg-Leesville, S.C. Soon after entering the college she was compelled to resign because of illness which continued over a lengthy period of time. During this period she was under the care of her aunt, Dr. Sophia Davis in Augusta, Ga. After her physical condition improved she returned home to serve as housekeeper for her father (a widower) while her brother and older sisters were engaged in other occupations. On 23 June 1914 she married Joseph Earle Steadman, and they lived consecutively in Edgefield County, S.C., Greenwood, S.C., Charleston, S.C., Washington, D.C., Hyattsville, Md., and again in Washington, D.C. She died in George Washington University Hospital in Washington and was buried in Edgewood Cemetery at Greenwood, S.C. In 1983 her remains were removed to the cemetery at Emory United Methodist Church in Saluda County.

Sallie and Earle were the parents of: — Samuel Francis (died in infancy), Sarah Louise (married Charles Dinsmore Wagner and had issue), Joseph Earle, Jr. (married Bernadette Katherine Hardy and had issue), James Henry (died in infancy), and Meldred Elizabeth (married Floyd William Taylor and had issue).

BUZHARDT

Jacob Buzhardt (ca. 1750; 1812) came from Germany to South Carolina in 1768. It is not known whether he came alone or in company with his parents. At about 1773 he married Ann Margaret _____ (ca. 1755; 1817), who also came from Germany in the same year, and they settled in the Dutch Fork of the present Newberry County. — (Information given by their descendants.) He was erroneously listed in the 1790 and 1800 censuses, respectively, as Jacob Busert and Jacob Buzzard. His will (dated 14 January 1809 and proved in 1812) and estate papers show his surname as Buzhart or Buzhardt. —

Zebulon DeLoache

Zebulon DeLoache's Children

(Newberry County, S.C., Wills: - Vol. 2, 1805-1826, Book F, p. 69.) The will of his wife is recorded on page 70 of the same volume and book.

On 12 March 1812 Jacob deeded 300 acres of land to his son Philip Buzhardt, — (Newberry County, S.C., Deed Book K, p. 208.)

The will of Jacob Buzhardt names his wife Margaret and children (not in order of birth): — Philip (born about 1777; named as executor; md. Mary Sligh.), Jacob (1774; 1854; named as executor; md. Elizabeth Sligh.), Elizabeth (1780; ca. 1865; md. James Wright, which see.), Gasper (md. _____ McNeill.), and Mary. The will also names his grandson Thomas Write/Wright (son of daughter Elizabeth).

HOWELL

In the early 1700s one Thomas Howell migrated from Monmouthshire, England, to Glamorganshire, Wales, and from thence came to America at about 1726. He settled in what now is New Kent County, Del., where he acquired large holdings of land and became a man of influence. Some of his children moved to New Jersey, where a number of them became prominent in public affairs. Descendants of this immigrant are living today in various parts of the United States. — (Ruby Haskins Ellis - Who Are You?)

Prior to or during the Revolutionary War one William Howell (born about 1729), believed to be a son or grandson of the above mentioned Thomas Howell, came to old Edgefield County, S.C., presumably from New Jersey. He evidently was the father of William Howl/Howell, Jr. (1753; lvg. 1833), Nathaniel Howell (born about 1756), and Thomas H. Howle/Howell (born about 1763), all of whom were American soldiers during the Revolutionary War. These men and their father (William Howl/Howell, Sr.) were separately listed in the 1790 census for Edgefield County, and all of them were slave holders. William, Sr., then had living with him two males and three females who evidently were his wife and younger children. The oldest son among these younger children was Josiah H. Howell (see following).

Josiah H. Howell (1770; 15 December 1851) was born in New Jersey and came to Edgefield County with his parents prior to or during the Revolutionary War. He was included in the 1800-1850 censuses for that county. In the latter year he, then being blind, was living in the home of his son-in-law Jacob Wright (which see) whose wife was Ann/Nancy Virginia Howell (see following).

On 27 July 1794 Josiah married Phoebe Humphries/Humphreys or Humphrey (which see). On 17 December 1796 he bought from John Mobley, Sr., 338 acres of land situated on Penn Creek waters of Little Saluda River in Edgefield (now Saluda) County, S.C. — (Deed Book 13, p. 519.) This apparently was the first land which he acquired, and settled there after having lived elsewhere. He and his wife were the parents of eleven children (all named in the Howell family Bible): — Kiturah (born 23 August 1795; md. John Humphries), — William (born 13 November 1797; md. Celia Humphries), — Daniel (born 16 January 1800), — Ira (born 18 January 1802), — Mary (born 23 March 1804; md. John Wright as his second wife), — Ann/Nancy Virginia (3 March 1806; 25 May 1890; md. Jacob Wright), — Josiah H. (born 8 March 1808; md. Sarah Eidson), — Catherine (born 1 May 1810; md. James Wright, Jr.), — Tresea (born 23 August 1812), — Jane (born 23 April 1815; md. John Wright as his first wife), — Phoebe (born 18 October 1820; unmarried). Information concerning the marriages of these children was furnished by the late Henry Thomas Wright, a descendant. Josiah's wife (Phoebe) died on 15 October 1847.

On 29 December 1827 Josiah Howell was named as one of the trustees to whom land was deeded by William Foy for the Methodist Episcopal Church (now Gassoway United Methodist Church) on a branch of Red Bank Creek, waters of Little Saluda River. — (The Edgefield Advertiser, issue of 12 July 1939). Josiah and his wife were among the organizers and long-time members of Bethlehem Methodist Church, which was established in August 1836. — (Hamlin Etheredge — Bethlehem's Spiritual Empire, pp. 7 and 9.) Both of these churches are situated in the present Saluda County, S.C.

HUMPHRIES

This family name appears in the records with various forms of spelling, such as: — Humphries, Humphreys, and Humphrey. On 7 August 1770 the Council of Colonial South Carolina approved the petition of William Humphreys, who had recently arrived in the province from Ireland (?), for a grant of 100 acres of land. The size of the grant (100 acres) indicates that, under governing rules, William then was an unmarried man or the head of a family. Since he came alone, and there is no record of a family for him who came as immigrants earlier or later than he, his marital status at that time is confirmed. — (Council Journal entry of even date.) No search has been made by this writer for a record of the grant, but it is believed that the land was situated in old Ninety Six District (later Edgefield and now Saluda County), S.C. During the period of 1786-1792 he was granted a total of 1,414 acres of land situated partly on Mine Creek and partly on Red Bank Creek in Ninety Six District. — (Land Grant Books and Land Plat Books in the State Archives at Columbia, S.C.)

Edgefield County records examined by this writer show that during the period of 1784-1796 William bought 622 acres of land from other persons. The deeds for this land show that it was situated partly on Dry Creek, partly on Mine Creek, and partly on Red Bank Creek. This together with the land which he acquired by grant gave him a total of at least 2,036 acres, of which he sold 1,220 acres. Since he died intestate it is assumed that the remaining 816 acres were sold and the proceeds divided among his heirs.

During the Revolutionary War William Humphries/Humphreys served as an American soldier in Captain William Butler's Company of South Carolina Volunteer Militia from Edgefield District. — (Revolutionary War Records in the National Archives, Washington, D.C. — Miscellaneous South Carolina Records, Folder 9; Sarah Sullivan Ervin - South Carolinians in the Revolution, p. 118.)

At about 1770 William Humphries (ca. 1747; 1797) married Ann/Nancy Roland (ca. 1753; lvg. 1800) who probably was a daughter of the John Rolen/Roland (which see) included in the 1790 census for Orangeburg District (South Part), S.C. He (William **Humphes**) was included in the 1790 census for Edgefield County and Ann, then a widow, was included in the 1800 census for that county. They were parents of the following listed children. — (Estate Papers, Box 4, Pack 1552, in the Probate Judge's Office at Edgefield, S.C.; Hamlin Etheridge — Bethlehem's Spiritual Empire, pp. 9 and 19.)

    1. Sarah (ca. 1771; ca. 1805). — Md. Richard Buffington as his first wife.

    2. Jane (ca. 1772; lvg. 1802). — Unmarried.

    3. Samuel (ca. 1774; 1826). — Md. Eunice Satcher.

    4. Phoebe (ca. 1775; 15 October 1847). — Md. Josiah H. Howell (which see).

    5. Mary (ca. 1777; ca. 1805). — Md. James Eidson as his first wife.

    6. Elizabeth (ca. 1778;   ). — Md. Robert Bouleware.

    7. Nancy (ca. 1780;   ). — Md. Spencer Boulware.

    8. William (ca. 1782; ca. 1850). — Unmarried.

    9. Roland (ca. 1784; 1814). — Md. Rachel Pou.

  10. Catherine (ca. 1787;   ) — Md. James Foy.

MATHENY
(Formerly Mathenay)

During 1934-1936 this writer received from William Blake Matheny (then a student at the University of Pennsylvania and later a student of law) data on the Matheny family in Europe. He had spent much time in research on this family, and had conducted a correspondence with Baron Albin Pidoux de la Madura who was the author of two books on the French nobility. The following paragraph is a very brief summary of Mr. Matheny's data on this ancient family of France.

The Matheny family originated in Franche - Comte (Department of Jura, France), which then was part of the Kingdom of Burgundy. It took its name from the Seigneurie (Lordship) de Mathenay, which it possessed from the 11th until the 15th century. It is a branch of the very ancient and venerable family of de Vaudrey, who had the titles Chevalier, Baron, Comte, and Marquis. The Mathenay family branches off from the de Vaudrey family after the year 1095 but before the year 1200. The de Vaudrey arms and the Mathenay arms are almost identical, and the two lordships are about five miles apart. The arms of the family "de Mathenay" of Franche - Comte (Jura), France, are shown in Volume 2 of Rietstap's "Amorial Genéral".

Upon the rise of Protestantism in France members of the Mathenay family affiliated with the Huguenots; and, in order to escape persecution by the Roman Catholic Church, some of them fled to England and to other European countries. A descendant of one of these refugees came from England to America during the middle 1600s and founded the family of which this sketch is the subject. The following data shown for persons in generations 1 through 5 was furnished to this writer by William Blake Matheny and William Porter Matheny, the latter being head of the history department at the Terrill School in Dallas, Texas.

Gen. 1. William Mettenye/Mathenay (born about 1600) of County Kent, England, and his family apparently were members of a Flemish Huguenot Church in that country. Among his children was a son named Daniel (see following). It is believed that another son was named Michael Mettaney/Mathenay.

Gen. 2. Daniel Mettenye/Mathenay (ca. 1638; ca. 1689) was born in England and died in Stafford County, Va. At about 1660 he and the forementioned Michael Mettaney/Mathenay came to Surry or Isle of Wight County, Va. In 1663 he went to Charles County, Md., and bought 300 acres of land there. — (Abstract of a Charles County deed in Maryland Historical Society, Baltimore, Md.; Charles County Court records transcribed in the Calvert County copy of the Rent Rolls.) Maryland records show his surname variously spelled as: — Macheny, Mathenya, Mathenia, Mathena, Methenia, or Methena. On 5 August 1664 he purchased from Thomas Wentworth a plantation called "Wentworth Woodhouse", which was the name of the Wentworth family estate in England. — (Charles County Deeds, Liber B. -1, folio 255.) He subsequently acquired other lands in Charles County, and established his home at Mattawoman on a tract which he patented under the name "Mathena's Folly".

In 1681 he was one of the leaders in a Protestant uprising against the Roman Catholics in the Colony of Maryland. On failure of the uprising he moved across the Potomac River to Stafford County, Va., where in 1683 he bought a plantation ("The Hope") on Acquia Creek adjoining the home of Colonel George Mason. This plantation remained in possession of the Matheny family until 1756, when the family moved into the Shenandoah Valley and scattered to other parts.

At about 1663-5 Daniel married Sarah Wentworth (presumably a daughter or sister of Thomas Wentworth) who survived him. They were the parents of four children, the oldest of whom was William Wentworth Matheney (see following).

Gen. 3. William Wentworth Matheney/Matheny (ca. 1666; Nov. 1705) was born in Charles County, Md., and died in Stafford County, Va., where his will (dated 12 November 1705) is of record. On 11 March 1690 he was appointed constable for the Stafford County precincts on Potomac Creek. In 1691 he married Mrs. Frances Mason (widow of Colonel George Mason), and they became the parents of four children, the oldest of whom was Daniel Matheny (see following).

Gen. 4. Daniel Matheny (ca. 1693; ca. 1747) was born and died in Stafford County, Va. He lived on the plantation ("The Hope") which descended to his father and which his father left to him. At about 1719 he married Mary _____ (died 12 January 1750), and they became the parents of six children among whom was James Matheny (see following). The Overwharton Parish register mentions two of his children who died, respectively, on 4 November and 24 November 1745. Overwharton Parish was in Stafford County.

Gen. 5. James Matheny (ca. 1725; bef. 1790) was born in Stafford County, Va., and died in Orangeburgh District (South Part - later Barnwell District), S.C. On 12 December 1751, at Overwharton Church in Stafford County, he married Elizabeth Gains. In 1757 he moved with other members of his father's family to the Shenandoah Valley of Virginia, from whence he moved to South Carolina prior to the Revolutionary War. During that war he served in the 5th Regiment of South Carolina Troops on the Continental Establishment. In 1782-3 he rendered patriotic service by ferrying continental troops and militia troops across a local stream of water. — (Revolutionary War Records in the National Archives at Washington, D.C.; Alexander S. Salley, Jr. — Stub Entries to Indents for Revolutionary Claims in South Carolina, Lib. O, indent No. 184; Revolutionary War Records in the State Archives at Columbia, S.C., File AA4827½.) His widow, Elizabeth Mathueny (died before 1800) and some of their children are included in the 1790 census for Orangeburgh District (South Part).

James and Elizabeth (Gains) Matheny were the parents of nine known children, four of whom went with them to Orangeburgh District (South Part), S.C., namely: — Mary (unmarried), Daniel (see following), Charles, and William. The five other children settled in various counties of Western Virginia.

Gen. 6. Daniel Mathaey (ca. 1765; 1816) was born in the Shenandoah Valley of Virginia, and went with his parents to Orangeburgh District (South Part), S.C., prior to the Revolutionary War. At the time of the 1790 census for that district his sister Mary and brother Charles apparently were living with him, while his brother William was living with their mother. At about 1792 he married Elizabeth _____ (living 1820), perhaps a daughter or sister of Hansford Duncan who was one of the bondsmen for the administration of Daniel's estate. In 1799 he was granted a tract of land situated on Grape Vine Creek near the present towns of Bamberg and Denmark, S.C. — (Grant Book 43, p. 328; Plat No. 14 in Bundle 116.) This probably was in addition to land which he previously had bought.

Daniel was included in the 1800 and 1810 censuses for Barnwell County, S.C., which (together) show that he was the father of six children and the owner of slaves. On 25 October 1816 administration papers on his estate were granted to his widow and son John Matheny. — (Estate papers at Barnwell Courthouse: — Bundle 27, Pack 3.) His children were: — Daughter (born about 1793), — John F. (ca. 1795; ca. 1837, — md. Rachel Guess), — William (ca. 1797; 1844, — md. Priscilla _____), — Daniel, Jr. (see following), — Daughter (born about 1801), — Charles (ca. 1804; ca. 1855, — md. Levicy/Louisa _____).

Gen. 7. Daniel Matheny, Jr. (ca. 1799; 1864) was born in Orangeburgh District (South Part - later Barnwell District), S.C., and died in the present town of Williston, S.C. At about 1823 he married Ann/Nancy _____ (died 17 May 1857) and settled in the area between Grape Vine Creek and Little Salkehatchie River, a few miles southwest of the present town of Bamberg. They probably became members of Springtown Baptist Church, which was located within that area. He was included in the 1830 census for Barnwell County.

At about 1838 he moved to Edgefield County, S.C., and settled in the neighborhood of Dry Creek Baptist Church (near the present towns of

Ward and Johnston), of which he, his wife, and children became members. He was included in the 1840 and 1850 censuses for Edgefield County, and then was a farmer, a blacksmith, and a slave owner.

After his wife's death, on 26 September 1858 Daniel requested and received a letter of dismissal from Dry Creek Baptist Church, of which he was a deacon, and went to the forementioned town of Williston (in Barnwell County), where he lived until the time of his death. His estate was administered by his son-in-law, Julius Pickens Wright, to whom letters were issued on 30 September 1864. — (Estate Papers at Edgefield County Courthouse: — File 89, Pack. 3574.) He and his wife were the parents of: — Catherine (born about 1824; md. Henry B. Raborn), — Jane (1 January 1826; 12 September 1856, - md. Julius Pickens Wright), — Charles R. (see following).

Gen. 8. Charles R. Matheny (ca. 1831; 19 August 1859) was born in Barnwell (now Bamberg) County, S.C. At about 1838 he went with his parents to Edgefield County, S.C.

On 6 February 1851 he married Eleanor/Ellen Jane Wright (7 May 1832; 11 March 1914), daughter of Jacob and Ann/Nancy Virginia Wright (which see). They apparently settled on the land which belonged to his father.

On 28 August 1853 Charles became a member of Dry Creek Baptist Church. After having been a member of Bethlehem Methodist Church, on 26 October 1755 Ellen became a member of the same church as was her husband. Both of these churches now are in the present Saluda County, S.C. On their deaths he was buried (grave now unmarked) in the cemetery at the Dry Creek Church and she was buried in the cemetery at the Bethlehem Church.

Letters of administration on the estate of Charles R. Matheny were issued to his father (Daniel Matheny, Jr.) on 10 October 1859. — (Estate Papers at Edgefield County Courthouse: — File 80, Pack. 3199.) He and his wife were the parents of: — Mary Alice (24 October 1852; 10 August 1892; — md. Zebulon DeLoache, which see), — Thomas Pope (born ca. 1854; md. 1st Mary Elizabeth Calhoun and 2nd Sarah Cicelle Calhoun), — Daniel Puckett (13 February 1856; 10 January 1931, - md. Mary Elizabeth/Betty Rushton), — Nancy Jane (ca. 1858; died in infancy), — Margaret/Maggie Anne (1859; 19   , - md. Thomas Edwards).

Eleanor/Ellen Jane Matheny, widow of Charles R. Matheny, was included in the 1860-1880 censuses for Edgefield County as head of a family. In the latter year her mother (Nancy Wright) was living with her. She died in the home of her son, Daniel Puckett Matheny. It was said of her: - ''She was a devout Christian, a true homemaker, a faithful friend, sympathetic, social, and generous; and no one ever heard her knowingly speak an unkind word to any living soul.''

ROLAND

It is claimed that this family descends both from Charlemagne and from his sister's son Roland. The ancestry of these men is traced through the following generations.

1. Pepin de Landen, an Austrasian nobleman and Mayor of the Palace during the reign of several kings of the Franks, died in 655 and was succeeded as mayor by his grandson Pepin de Heristal (see following). Austrasia was an ancient kingdom in Midwestern Europe under the Merovingian line of kings of the Franks. Pepin was the father of an only child, a daughter —

2. Becga, who married Adelgisel, son of Arnulph (Bishop of Metz), and had —

3. Pepin de Heristal (ca. 630; 714). He was Major-domo at the court of King Dagobert II. After the king's death in 688 he was appointed Duke of the Franks, and ruled the kingdom with so much justice that he was enabled to make his office hereditary in his family. By Alfraida he was the father of —

4. Charles Martel (ca. 690; 741). From 714 until 737, as Mayor of the Palace, he was the acting head of the government of the Kingdom of the Franks during the reign of three slothful and indifferent kings. From 737 to 741 he ruled the kingdom alone. In 732 he overthrew the Saracens at Tours, from which he acquired the name of Martel (signifying hammer). In 741 he bequeathed his hereditary office to his sons Pepin (see following) and Carolman. Pepin was a son of Charles' first wife (name not given).

5. Pepin (ca. 714; 768) was called **Pepin le Bref** (the Short) because of his short stature. Soon after the death of their father Carloman (died in 770) entered a convent, and Pepin assumed all of the benefits of the hereditary office which had been bequeathed to the two brothers. He was Mayor of the Palace from 741 until 751. In the latter year, by agreement of the pope, he was proclaimed King of the Franks and reigned as such until the time of his death. During the period of 751 - 756 he defeated the Lombards in Italy, and made the Holy See a present of the lands which he conquered from them, — this being the origin of the temporal power of the popes. He was the founder of the Carlovingian dynasty of kings. By his wife Berta/Bertrade (called **Bertha of the Big Foot**), daughter of Count Laon of Neustria, he was the father of Charles (see following) and a daughter (see following) whose name has not been learned by this writer.

6-1. Charles (742; 814), called Charles the Great, or Charlemagne, succeeded his father as King of the Franks and reigned as such during the period of 768-800. Early in his reign he began a war with the Saxons which, with many interruptions, lasted more than thirty years (772-803). The conquered Saxons accepted Christianity and the firm, just rule of Charlemagne. At an interval of quiet during the war, in 778, he invaded Spain in a campaign against the Saracens. The campaign was a failure, and the baggage-train and many men were lost as the army fell into an ambuscade while retreating through a gorge at Roncesvalles. Among the officers killed was his nephew Roland (see following). On Christmas Day in 800 Pope Leo III crowned him Emperor of the Romans, which in one sense was a revival of the Roman Empire of the West. He ruled as emperor until the time of his death. From the fact that he stamped his character upon Western Europe and gave direction to the current of its history for centuries, he is reckoned among the most eminent men of all time. His eldest son was Charles (see following).

6-2. _____ (name not learned), daughter of Pepin le Bref and sister of Charlemagne, was the mother of a son named **Roland** (see following)

7-1. Charles, son of Charlemagne, was made Duke of Engleheim/Ingleheim by his father. Ingleheim, an estate near Frankfort (on the Rhine River) in the ancient Kingdom of Austrasia, was a favorite residence of Charlemagne. Charles married Juliana (see following), a daughter of his first cousin (Roland).

7-2. Roland (died 778), son of a daughter of Pepin le Bref and nephew of Charlemagne, was also called **Orlando**. He was a hero of the romances of chivalry, and one of the paladians of his uncle. He was a brave and loyal warrior. The old French epics "Song of Roland", "Orlando Inamorato", and "Orlando Furioso" relate to him. His daughter Juliana (see following) married Charles, Duke of Ingleheim, her father's first cousin.

8. Charles (son of Charlemagne and Duke of Ingleheim) and Juliana (daughter of Roland) apparently had a son **Roland**, through whom the subject family claims descent both from Charlemagne and the first Roland.

References

An Ancient History for Beginners. — G.W. Botsford.

History of All Nations, Vol. II. — S.G. Goodrich.

Outlines of the World's History. — William Swinton.

Six Thousand Years of History, Vol. VI. — Edgar Sanderson, et. al.

The American International Encyclopedia, Vols. IV, XII, and XIII.

The New Century Dictionary — DeLuxe Edition, 1952.

The Noble Lineage of the Delaware - West Family of Virginia. — Ann Woodward Fox.

Webster's New International Dictionary - 1915 Edition.

Of particular interest to this writer is the ancestry of Ann/Nancy Roland who at about 1770 married William Humphries (which see) in South Carolina. As heretofore stated, it is believed that she was a daughter of the John Rolen/Roland included in the 1790 census for Orangeburgh District (South Part), S.C. It is believed that John (born about 1728), probably a migrant from Virginia, was the father also of Edward Rolin/Roland (born about 1752) and David Roland (born about 1763) who were included in the same census for Orangeburgh District. (David was twice listed in that census, probably because of having moved from one location to another. In 1800 he was included in the census for the adjoining Edgefield County, S.C., where in 1801 he bought land which he sold in 1803. — Deed Book 24, pp. 1 and 90. — His wife was named Mary/Polly.) — Another probable son of John was John Rolan or Rowland/Roland, Jr.? (born about 1766) who in 1788 bought land in Edgefield County and was included in the 1790 census for that county.

His widow Rachel Rolen/Roland, with two young sons and two uniden-
tified females living with her, was included in the 1800 census for
Edgefield County. A third son, evidently a posthumous child, was born
soon after the 1800 census was taken. In 1815 these three sons
(Zachariah, William, and John), his only lawful heirs and representatives, sold the said land to Daniel Ward. — (Deed Book 37, p. 117;
Deed Book 47, p. 369.) — It is probable that this Roland Family of
Orangeburgh District and Edgefield County was closely related to some
or all of the Roland families in Laurens County, S.C., where the given
names Zachariah, William, and John appear in records of the time.

The descendants of Ann/Nancy (Roland) Humphries, in speaking of
her children state that they were of French descent. Besides a son named
Roland Humphries, many of her descendants of the past were and of the
present are known by the given name of Roland.

From Janie Revill's "Compilation of Original Lists of Protestant Immigrants to South Carolina, 1763-1773", pages 16 through 25, it is noted
that one Piere/Peter Rolland/Roland, a French Protestant (Huguenot)
from the southern part of France, arrived in Charleston, S.C., where his
petition for land and bounty was approved on 18 April 1764. The land
assigned to him was in Bordeau Township (now in Abbeville County) of
the province, but until the spring of 1765 he resided at Fort Lyttleton
near the Atlantic Coast. It apparently was he (Peter Rowland/Roland)
who later settled in Pendleton District (now Anderson County), S.C.,
where he was included in the 1790 census.

WRIGHT

Thomas Wright of Belfast, Ireland, came to Charleston, S.C., in the
year 1773, bringing his wife and children with him. — (Family Bible
record of his son James Wright and information given by James' grandson James Russell Wright and grandson Beauford Wallace Wright.)
Soon after his arrival in South Carolina he settled in Saint Marks Parish,
which in 1768 became known also as Camden Judicial District of old
Craven County, S.C. This parish, or district, was the section of country
lying between Broad River and Lynches Creek. Thomas apparently lived
near Broad River, across from the present Newberry County, S.C.,
where he died about the year 1775. The will of Thomas Wright, - 13 October 1775, - of Saint Marks Parish, Craven County, is recorded in the
courthouse at Charleston, S.C. - (Will Book 1774-1779, p. 435, - or Vol.
17, Book B, p. 583.) The will mentions his wife Mary, and sons Thomas
and James (see following). The son Thomas moved to Newberry County,
where he died at about 1820 leaving at least seven children: - Thomas,
Jr., Margaret, Elizabeth, Jacob, James, John, and Elvira. In 1829
Thomas, Jr., gave bond as guardian of his brothers and sisters. -
(Records in office of Newberry County Clerk of Court - Index to Litiga-
tions: - Box 3, Packs 24 and 25 and Box 80, Pack 55.)

James Wright (1767; 20 January 1855) was born in Ireland and in
1773, at the age of six years, he came to Charleston, S.C., with his
parents. - (Family Bible record, etc., as above.) It apparently was he

(James Right) who at the time of the 1790 census, being then unmarried, was living in the Dutch Fork Section of old Orangeburgh District (North Part - now Lexington County), S.C. A part of this section was later incorporated into Newberry County, S.C. At about 1799-1800 he married Elizabeth/Betsy Buzhardt (which see) and lived in the Dutch Fork of Newberry County until his removal to Edgefield County, S.C., prior to or during 1816. On 10 January 1816 James Wright of Edgefield County deeded to Robert Park of Newberry a tract of land which he (Wright) had acquired on 19 November 1813. - (Newberry County, S.C., Deed Book L, p. 199.) He subsequently was included in the 1820 census for Edgefield County. His age is erroneously stated in the 1840 and 1850 censuses.

When James Wright moved to Edgefield County, he acquired and settled on land situated on waters of Rocky Creek, where he lived until the time of his death. - (In 1860 his widow was living with her widowed daughter, Margaret Matthews, in the Fruit Hill section of Edgefield County.) - In 1831 he and his wife became members of Rocky Creek Baptist Church, and (presumably) they are buried in the cemetery at that place. During many years prior to his death he engaged in hauling goods from Boston, Mass., to Hamburg and Edgefield, S.C. In his absence from home one of his older sons took charge of the farming operations and other affairs. - (Information given by his descendants, James Russell Wright and Henry Thomas Wright.)

Family Bible and census records show that James and Elizabeth (Buzhardt) Wright were the parents of ten children: - Thomas (1800; 1826, - Md. Frances Goodwyn and had issue), Margaret (1803; lvg. 1860, - md. Mark Matthews and had issue), Elizabeth (1804; 1865, - md. Young J. Goodwyn and had issue), Jacob (see following), Henry (1807?; 1817), James (1809; 1846, - md. Catherine/Kate Howell and had issue), Amanda (ca. 1811; bef. 1830), John (1813; 1882, - md. 1st Jane Howell and 2nd Mary/Polly Howell, sisters, and had issue), William (1816?; 1819?), and Emeline (1819; 1849, - md. Henry B. Rabon).

Jacob Wright (19 June 1805; 15 June 1863) was born in Newberry County, S.C., and died at his home (still standing in 1955) near Bethlehem Methodist Church in the present Saluda (formerly Edgefield) County, S.C. He is buried in a family graveyard on the plantation where he lived from the time of his marriage until the time of his death. His wife and one of his children (John W.) also are buried there. On 15 July 1827 he married Ann/Nancy Virginia Howell (which see). In August 1836 they were among the organizers of the Bethlehem Methodist Church in Edgefield (now Saluda) County, and remained in its membership until the time of their deaths. — (Hammond Etheridge - Bethlehem's Spiritual Empire, p. 7.) They were the parents of thirteen children: - Kiturah/Kitty May (born ca. 1828, md. Floyd Whittle and had issue), Thomas C. (ca. 1830; 1864, - unmd.), Eleanor (7 May 1832; 11 March 1914, - md. Charles R. Matheny, which see), Josiah H. (ca. 1834; 1862, - unmd.), William H. (1835; 1911, - md. Lucinda Turner and had issue), Ira B. (ca. 1836; 1911, - md. _____ and had issue), John Wesley (1838; 1864, - unmd.), Anna P. (1839; lvg. 1914, - md. Amos W. Satcher and had issue), James Russell (1841; lvg. 1914, - md. 1st Frances Powers and had issue; md. 2nd Mrs. Fannie Smiley and had no issue), Jacob Fletcher (ca. 1842; 1931, - md. Carrie Jennings and had issue), Nancy Virginia/Jennie (ca. 1843;   ; - md. Jesse Timmerman and had issue), Alvin Curtis (ca. 1844; bef. 1932, - md. _____ Richards and had issue), and Robert S. (1848; 1911, - md. Lavinia Cogburn and had issue). - (Census records and information given by descendants.)

SKETCH NO. 8
JAMES NATHANIEL DeLOACHE

James/Jim Nathaniel DeLoache (28 October 1879; 5 October 1967). — He was born at the homestead established by his grandfather. In later years he acquired a part of the land on which the homestead was located, and built a house in which he lived until the time of his death. He was educated at the forementioned Emory High School (See SKETCH NO. 7) and at Leesville College (Leesville, S.C.). During 1900-1906 he taught school in Saluda County, S.C., and during 1907 - 1908 he was the County Superintendent of Education. From 1 April 1911 to 30 April 1935 he served as County Treasurer, holding that office longer than any one of his predecessors. The following item, published in The National Observer - October 1, 1935, attests the superior quality of his service in the office of treasurer.

J.N. DeLOACH

"It is most important at this time, we feel, to direct attention to the manner in which county governments are functioning after the years of the depression.

"There is nothing which adds so much to the welfare of the people in general as to know that their county governments are being operated in a manner that is most economical and efficient therein.

"With this thought in mind we are pleased to present to our readers the excellent work being done by J.N. DeLoach, County Treasurer of Saluda County in the State of South Carolina.

"The problems that confront the county treasurer of this county are about similar to those which other counties face, the strengthening of the county's financial structure, the enhancement of its bonds in the open market, the reduction of current expenditures, and the functioning of its various departments in the most efficient manner possible.

"Mr. DeLoach is well known as a sound and capable business man with a keen knowledge of existing business conditions and he has applied constructive policies in his administration of the post he holds and which have been reflected in the steady improvement of the county's financial status."

During the period of 1940-1958 he served as secretary for Palmetto Hosiery Mill, Incorporated, in the town of Saluda. As an activity concurrent with duties performed in the positions and offices which he held, he carried on farming operations in which he had a lifelong interest.

He was a lifelong and faithful member of the Methodist Church, being first associated with what now is Emory United Methodist Church (located near the Emory High School which he attended) and later with Saint Paul United Methodist Church in the town of Saluda. In one or the other of these churches he served in the various offices of steward, trustee, Sunday school teacher, or Sunday school superintendent. One of the Sunday school classes at Saint Paul was named in his honor. There was much about him which reminded one of the Christian life and character of his father.

On 25 June 1913 he married Mary Elizabeth Lester (4 March 1885; 14 April 1971), daughter of George B. and Susan Catherine (Kempson) Lester. She was a graduate of Newberry College (Newberry, S.C.), and taught school (Bethany and Corinth) in Saluda County before her marriage. Jim and Mary are buried in Travis Park Cemetery in the town of Saluda. They were the parents of the following named children, all of whom are living in 1981.

1. James Lester (8 May 1914;   ). - Unmarried. He graduated from Clemson College (now University) at Clemson, S.C. He served in the Second World War, and subsequently entered the United States Army Reserve from which he retired with the rank of lieutenant colonel. He now lives in Carboro, N.C., where he has real estate interests.

2. Michael Kempson (12 January 1916;   ). - He graduated from Wofford College (Spartanburg, S.C.). He served in the Second World War, and subsequently entered the United States Army Reserve from which he retired with the rank of colonel. During a number of years he held an official position with Bankers Trust of South Carolina in the town of Saluda. Now retired, he lives in Saluda County. He is unmarried.

3. Mary Susan (11 June 1917;   ). - She graduated from Furman University (Greenville, S.C.) and Tulane University (New Orleans, La.) and engaged in teaching and professional social work. Now retired, she lives in Saluda County. She is unmarried.

4. Paul Matheny (31 May 1919;   ). - He attended Newberry College (Newberry, S.C.). He served in the Second World War as a Staff Sergeant, Military Police Platoon, attached to the 30th Infantry Division of the United States Army. He is an executive with Saluda Finance Corportion in the town of Saluda. On 29 January 1953 he married Lois Kaiser of Lexington County, S.C. They live in Saluda County, and are the parents of: **FRANK** (graduated from University of South Carolina in Columbia, S.C.; married Mary Katherine Kevin; living in Saint Petersburg, Fla.). — **MICHAEL** (graduated from Newberry College in Newberry, S.C.; unmarried; living in Saluda County, S.C.). — **SUSAN** (student at University of South Carolina in Columbia, S.C.; living in Saluda County, S.C.; unmarried).

5. Ruth (30 May 1923;   ). - She graduated from Spartanburg Methodist College (Spartanburg, S.C.). On 6 October 1945 she married Fletcher Dew Thompson, and they became the parents of: — Jennie Lee, Rebecca Lynn, Laurie Kay, and James Fletcher Thompson. Ruth and Fletcher now live at Moore (Route 1), Spartanburg, S.C.

6. Dora Elizabeth (13 February 1927;   ). - She attended Erskine College (Due West, S.C.). On 31 May 1947 she married Sidney Bowles Hare, and they became the parents of: — Mary Elizabeth, James Sidney, and John Herman Hare. Dora and Sidney now live in Saluda County, S.C. She is employed by the South Carolina Judicial Department.

7. Sarah Eugenia (15 April 1928;   ). - She graduated from Spartanburg Methodist College (Spartanburg, S.C.), received a Bachelor of Arts degree from Columbia College (Columbia, S.C.), and a Master of Arts degree from Emory University (Atlanta, Ga.). She was Director of

Christian Education at Trinity United Methodist Church in Sumter, S.C., and now is a teacher at Wilson Hall School in that city. On 27 June 1952 she married Edward Vause Gibson, and they became the parents of: — Frances Elizabeth and Dollie DeLoache Gibson. Sara and ''Ed'' now live in Sumter.

James Nathaniel DeLoache
and his wife
Mary Elizabeth Lester

Their Fiftieth Anniversary

The J.N. DeLoaches and Children

The J.N. DeLoaches' Grandchildren

Michael Kempson

George B. Lester and his wife, Susan Catherine Kempson

CONWILL

This family name has been spelled also as Conwell.

Bejamin Conwill settled in the area of Newberry County, S.C., prior to the Revolutionary War, in which he served as a private in the American army. — (O'Neall and Chapman—The Annals of Newberry, p. 62; George Leland Summer, Sr. — Newberry County, South Carolina, Historical and Genealogical, p. 9.) He was included in the 1790 census for Newberry County, and apparently died before 1816. He probably was a brother of James, John, Joseph, and William Conwill, who also were included in the said census. He married Rachel _____, and had children among whom were the following named.

1. Benjamin, Jr. — He was included in the 1790 census for Newberry County, S.C., and was mentioned in the estate papers of his brother John Conwill.

2. John (died 1816). — He died in Newberry County, S.C., and apparently was unmarried. His estate papers mention his mother Rachel, and brothers and sister.

3. Hosea (died in 1829).

4. Bailey. — See following.

5. Wilber.

6. Elizabeth. — She married John Rikard.

Bailey Conwill (died about 1845), a native of Newberry County, S.C., married Catherine _____ (survived her husband) and had children (all living in 1845): — Rebecca (married Benjamin D. Lake), Ellen, Mary Elizabeth (married Michael H. Kempson, — which see), Drayton (remembered by his great-niece, the late Mrs. Ada Eugenia Grigsby), and Amos. Information concerning him, and his brothers and sister, is contained in George Leland Summer, Sr's., Newberry County, South Carolina, Historical and Genealogical'', p. 326.

CREIGHTON

Hugh Creighton of Newberry County, S.C., died leaving a will (dated 5 August 1793 and proved on 21 October 1793) in which he mentioned his wife (not named), his children: — Mary (married _____ Ward), Anne (married John Dennis, — which see), other children when they come to proper age; and his grandchildren: — Creighton Ward, Mary Dennis, and Joel Dennis. He (Hugh Craton) was included in the 1790 census for Newberry County. — (George Leland Summer, Sr. — Newberry County, South Carolina, Historical and Genealogical, p. 462.)

DENNIS

John Dennis of Newberry County, S.C., served as a private in the American Army during the Revolutionary War. He was included in the 1790 census for the said county, and was living in the second house from his father-in-law Hugh Creighton (Craton). In 1799 he acquired 350 acres of land on Buffalo Creek in Newberry County. He married Anne Creighton (which see), and had a number of children among whom were: James (see following), Mary, and Joel. — (George Leland Summer, Sr. — Newberry County, South Carolina, Historical and Genealogical, pp. 10 and 332.)

James Dennis of Newberry County, S.C., married Prudence Hawkins (which see). He apparently predeceased her, and she died about 1847 leaving children: — Martha (married Allen Lester, — which see), Phoebe (married Honorias Sheppard), Jesse, Rebecca, and P.H. (Peter Hawkins) Dennis. — (O'Neall and Chapman — The Annals of Newberry, pp. 642-3; George Leland Summer, Sr. — Newberry County, South Carolina, Historical and Genealogical, pp. 277 and 332.)

HAWKINS

Peter Hawkins (died about 1800-2) and his wife Prudence, of English extraction, came from Virginia before the Revolutionary War and settled in the southern part of Newberry County, S.C. He served as a private in the American army during the war. He was included in the 1790 census for the said county. The children of this couple were: — Jacob, Edward, Peter, William, Prudence (married James Dennis, — which see) and Elizabeth (married _____ Rankin). — (O'Neall and Chapman — The Annals of Newberry, pp. 643-4; George Leland Summer, Sr. — Newberry County, South Carolina, Historical and Genealogical, p. 345.)

BOOZER

Ulrich Boozer (originally Buser), thought to be a Swiss or German immigrant to Pennsylvania, came to South Carolina before 1756 and perhaps as early as the late 1730s. On 1 January 1740 one Ann/Anna Buser married John Jacob Meyer in the church at Orangeburgh, and on 18 April 1756 Ulrich Booser (son of Ulrich, Sr.) was a surety at a baptism in the same church. — (Alexander S. Salley, Jr. — The History of Orangeburg County, pp. 95, 107, and 161.)

On his arrival in South Carolina Ulrich Boozer settled in the lower section of old Camden District which lay north of Santee River and east of old Orangeburgh District. Some of his sons later moved into Lexington County, and others into Newberry County. He was twice married (names of wives not learned), the first wife being the mother of George and Catherine. — The second wife was the mother of Jacob, John, Frederick, Henry (see following), Ulrich (settled in Orangeburg County, — see above), Gasper, and Rudolph. — (George Leland Summer, Sr. — Newberry County South Carolina, Historical and Genealogical, p. 195.)

Henry Boozer (died about 1837) married and settled in Newberry County, where he was included in the 1790 census. In 1828 he made a will in which he mentions his wife Elizabeth (died in 1845) and children: — David, Henry, Jr. (see following), Frederick, John, Sarah (married

Jacob Cappleman), Daniel, George, Elizabeth (married Daniel Senn), Adam, and Rebecca (married _____ Hendrix). — (Ibid.)

Henry Boozer, Jr. (died 22 February 1859) settled in Newberry County, where he died leaving as his legatees twelve children and three sets of grandchildren. The children were: — Samuel, Timothy, Rebecca (married William McCormick), Henry, John A., Daniel, William A., Frederick, David W., Andrew, Adam P., and Matthias Pinckney. Grandchildren: — Lodoska (daughter of deceased son George; married David Merchant), Allen, George, and Amanda Lester (children of deceased daughter Elizabeth Lester - which see), and Thomas and Permelia (children of deceased son Edward). — (Ibid.)

KEMPSON

This family name apparently is misspelled as **Kampton** or **Kempton** in the printed copy of the 1790 census for South Carolina. At that time one Samuel **Kampton** was living among the Quakers in Newberry County, with 7 males and 4 females included in his household. He probably came to South Carolina from Pennsylvania or Maryland, and perhaps was a close relative of one John Kempson who died in 1750 in Cecil County, Md., leaving two daughters: — Elizabeth (wife of George Simcoe) and Ann (wife of Richard Stedman). John Kempson, his daughters, and their husbands were members of the Quaker faith. — (Records in Land Office, Annapolis, Md. — Administration Accounts, Vol. 28, p. 133.) One of the sons of Samuel Kampton/Kempson apparently was Frederick Kempson (see following).

Frederick Kempson of Newberry County, S.C., and his wife (name not learned) were the parents of: — Michael H. (see following), Katie (married George Henry Long), Benjamin (married Ella Summer), Elizabeth (married Jefferson Kinard), and Annie Louisa (married Luther Buford Wheeler). — (The Family History of Saluda County, 1895-1980, p. 237.)

Michael H. Kempson (5 February 1829; 27 January 1929) was born in Newberry County, S.C. While living there he married Mary Elizabeth Conwill (which see), who was ten years younger than himself, and prior to 1859 they moved to Edgefield (now Saluda) County, S.C. He was one of the Edgefield County men who served as privates in Company K, Second Regiment Artillery, during the War Between the States. The said company was "enlisted" in August 1861 and surrendered with General Joe E. Johnston at Greensboro, N.C., in 1865. — (John A. Chapman — History of Edgefield County, South Carolina, pp. 499 and 500; The Family History of Saluda County, 1895-1980, p. 242.) He and his wife were the parents of: Fred H. (married 1. Cornelia Etheredge and 2. Kate Bouknight), Susan Catherine (married George B. Lester, - which see), Peter (married Margaret Sanders), Leila (married Walter Satcher), and Hattie (married Charlie Davis). — (Information given by the late Mrs. Ada Eugenia Grigsby, a granddaughter; The Family History of Saluda County, 1895-1980, pp. 237 and 242.) The 1880 census for Edgefield County, S.C., shows that Peter (aged 19 years), Leila/Lenora (aged 16 years), and Harriett/Hattie (aged 14 years) then were unmarried and living with their parents.

LESTER

The Norman-French family of Lester (in earlier times de Leicester, de Leycestre, or de Laycester) came to England from France with William the Conqueror in 1066. The family coat of arms is: — "Argent a fesse azure between 3 fleurs-de-lis gules. Crest: — a demi-griffin sergeant gules". — (The Norman People).

During the early colonial period five members of the Lester family immigrated from England to Virginia: — Thomas before 1622, James in 1637, Ralph in 1643, Robert in 1649, and Thomas in 1653. By the time of the Revolutionary War their descendants numbered fully twenty families in Virginia, besides others who had migrated to the Carolinas. — (Biographical History of Virginia; Makers of America.)

James Lester came to the present Newberry County, S.C., prior to or during 1760, bringing with him his wife (name not learned) and four sons: — Peter (died in 1808 leaving issue), James, Jr., Samuel, and Charles (see following). He was granted 350 acres of land, apparently in right of six persons (100 acres for himself and 50 acres each for five other persons) included in his family. Peter, James, Jr., and Charles served as privates with the Americans during the Revolutionary War. James (Sr.) died after 1808 leaving children (younger ones born in South Carolina): — James, Jr., Samuel (out of state; died in 1817; unmarried), Charles (out of state), John, Isaac, Joyce (married James Beaumont and predeceased her father), Abner (out of state), and Alfred (named in the will of his brother Charles). — (O'Neall and Chapman — The Annals of Newberry, p. 642; George Leland Summer, Sr. — Newberry County, South Carolina, Historical and Genealogical, pp. 9 and 358.)

Charles Lester born in Virginia, came to Newberry County, S.C., with his parents. He served in the American army throughout the Revolutionary War. — (O'Neall and Chapman — The Annals of Newberry, p. 642; George Leland Summer, Sr. — Newberry County, South Carolina, Historical and Genealogical, pp. 9 and 358.) He married a Miss Musgrove (which see), whose given name has not been learned. During the period before and/or after 1808 he lived out of the State of South Carolina, as is mentioned in his father's estate papers, but the place of his other residence and the time of his return to Newberry County have not been learned by this writer. His wife apparently predeceased him, and he died in 1827 leaving children: — Allen (see following), Smith (moved to Alabama), Alfred (moved to Alabama), Millbury (married Dempsey Gilbert), Maria (married George Boozer), and Susan (married Lacy Havird).

Allen Lester, probably born in Newberry County, S.C., served in Company C, Third Regiment, South Carolina Volunteers, during the War Between the States (1861-1865) and apparently was discharged because of age. — (O'Neall and Chapman — The Annals of Newberry, p. 425.) He married Martha Dennis (which see), and they became the parents of: — James (see following), Charles, William, George, Alfred, Martha (married Atwood Connelly), Prudence (married _____ Rogers), Phoebe (married Warren Kirkland), Rebecca, and Jane (married _____ Rikard). — (O'Neall and Chapman — The Annals of Newberry, p. 642; George Leland Summer, Sr. — Newberry County, South Carolina, Historical and Genealogical, p. 358.)

James Lester, born in Newberry County, S.C., doubtless served in the War Between the States, as his father and brothers did. The lists given in "The Annals of Newberry" are not complete for some of the companies, as stated on page 13 of George Leland Summer's book. His first wife was Elizabeth Boozer (which see), who was the mother of: — Allen M., George B. (see following), and Amanda (married _____ Nichols). The second wife was Polly Boozer, who was the mother of: — Newton, Elizabeth, and Fannie. — (O'Neall and Chapman — The Annals of Newberry, p. 642.)

George B. Lester (22 June 1851; 12 October 1933), born in Newberry County, moved to Saluda County, S.C., in 1884. He was a farmer. He was the first representative from Saluda County (formed in 1895) in the state legislature, serving the term of 1896-1898 and again during 1904-1908. In 1879 he married Susan Catherine Kempson (which see), who was born on 14 March 1859 and died on 18 March 1940. They were the parents of: —

1. James Monroe (1880; 1968). — He married and had issue.
2. Ada Eugenia (11 September 1881; 14 January 1979). — She married Jacob Levi Grigsby and had issue.
3. Michael Henry (; 1952). — He married Emma Catherine Black and had issue.
4. Mary Elizabeth (4 March 1885; 14 April 1971). — She married James Nathaniel DeLoache (which see) and had issue.
5. Fairy Sula (;   ). — She married Ernest Black and had issue.
6. Joel Allen (;   ). — Died young.
7. Hattie Lee (;   ). — She married Ira B. Cromley. No issue.
8. Annie Laura (;   ). — Unmarried.
9. Ida Peral (1893; 12 May 1974). — Unmarried.

Information concerning George B. Lester and his family was obtained from some of his children and from The Family History of Saluda County, 1895-1980, pp. 242-3.

MUSGROVE

Edward Musgrove (1716; 1792), a native of England, was one of the earliest settlers in the upper country of South Carolina. He acquired land and settled on the north side of Enoree River in the present Laurens County. He had received a good education, was trained in the law, and was a practical surveyor. He gave legal advice and drew legal papers for all who needed them. He was a man of many abilities, being hospitable and benevolent and of firm and decisive character. At an early date he built the noted "Musgrove Mills" at which a Revolutionary War battle was fought in 1780. He was buried in the small graveyard behind the site of his house and near to the mills. — (Draper — King's Mountain and Its Heroes, pp. 123-4.)

On 6 February 1760 Edward Musgrove, then a captain of militia on the Enoree River, wrote a letter to William Bull (royal governor of South

Carolina) concerning murders committed by the Cherokee Indians. At a later date he bore the rank of major. — (Names in South Carolina, Vol. XXIV, p. 10.) When the Revolutionary War commenced he was living with his third wife. He then was too old for active duty and remained neutral in his sympathies, but he prayed each night for a speedy return of peace and good will among men. His sons took an active part in the war, some fighting on the side of the British and some fighting on the side of the Americans. — (Draper — King's Mountain and Its Heroes, pp. 123-4; J.S. Bolick — A Laurens County Sketchbook, p. 10.)

He fathered children by each of his three wives, but the total number and pertinent dates have not been learned. His first wife apparently was a Miss Beeks (relative of Samuel Beeks/Beaks of the 1790 census for Newberry County, S.C.). She was the mother of several children, among whom were:

1. Edward, Jr. (mentioned as "Colonel"). — He apparently served with the Americans during the Revolutionary War. The Ann Musgrove and family included in the 1790 census for Laurens County probably were his widow and children.

2. John (mentioned as "Colonel"). — He married and settled on land near the Saluda River in Newberry County. His home was in the same general area in which the Lester, Conwill, and Dennis families lived. He served with the British during the Revolutionary War, after which he left South Carolina and probably went to Georgia. — (O'Neall and Chapman — The Annals of Newberry, pp. 50 and 63-4.)

3. Beeks. — He first served with the British and later with the Americans during the Revolutionary War. His claim for service with the Americans was audited and forwarded to a legislative committee for approval during the period of August 1783 - August 1786. He was included in the 1790 census for Laurens County, being then the head of a family. — (Draper-King's Mountain and Its Heroes, pp. 124-5; J.S. Bolick - A Laurens County Sketch Book, pp. 11 and 12; Revill — Revolutionary Claims in South Carolina, p. 252.)

The second wife of Major Edward Musgrove was a Miss Fancher, who was the mother of two daughters:

1. Mary (ca. 1755; ca. 1782). — She died unmarried. It was her plea that saved the life of her half brother Beeks Musgrove and resulted in his switch from the British to the American cause. — (Draper-King's Mountain and Its Heroes, pp. 124-6; J.S. Bolick — A Laurens County Sketch Book, pp. 11 and 12.)

2. Susan (ca. 1757; ca. 1783). — She died unmarried. She and three girl friends acted as pallbearers at the funeral of her sister Mary, this being in accordance with the sister's request. — (Draper-King's Mountain and Its Heroes, p. 126.)

The third wife of Major Edward Musgrove was living with him at the commencement of the Revolutionary War. She was the mother of the following named children who in 1796, at a sheriff's sale, sold land at Musgrove Mills. — (George Leland Summer, Sr. — Newberry County, S.C., — Historical and Genealogical, pp. 300 and 367.)

1. William — He was included in the 1790 census for Newberry County. By his father's will (Laurens County Will Book A, p. 28) he acquired "the dwelling plantation, mill, and all the land", with the stipula-

tion that his mother benefit from the proceeds from the property for the duration of her life. — (Names in South Carolina, Vol. XVII, p. 26.)

2. Margaret (1768; 1824). — She married Landon Waters. — (Draper - King's Mountain and Its Heroes, p. 126.)

3. Rachel. — Apparently unmarried in 1796.

4. Leah. — Apparently unmarried in 1796.

5. Linney. — Apparently unmarried in 1796.

A daughter of the first wife of Major Edward Musgrove or one of his granddaughters, — name not learned, — married Charles Lester (which see). — (O'Neall and Chapman — The Annals of Newberry, p. 642; George Leland Summer, Sr. — Newberry County, S.C. — Historical and Genealogical, p. 358.)

ERRATA

Page 3.   On 11th line, after references change the semicolon to a comma.

In 2nd paragraph, change Reitstap's to Rietstap's.

Page 4.   Faulty printing under the coat of arms should be DesLoges and Vs.

Page 9.   In 1st paragraph, change interstate to intestate.

In 2nd paragraph, change 1683 to 1680.

Page 27.   On 9th line, change names to name, and insert of one before unknown.

Page 29.   On 3rd line, change then to formerly.

Page 31.   On last line, change 374 to 375.

Page 34.   In item 3, insert a period after 1810).

Page 60.   In item 4, change Carolman to Carloman.

Page 74.   In item 9, change Peral to Pearl.

Page 50.   On 3rd line from bottom, change ALTER to ALTAR.

Page 58.   Gen. 6, on 1st line, change MATHHEY to MATHENY.

77

www.ingramcontent.com/pod-product-compliance
Lightning Source LLC
Chambersburg PA
CBHW062104270326
41931CB00013B/3207